# COLLINS GEM

# ENGLISH
## *School*
# THESAURUS

HarperCollins*Publishers*

First Published in this edition 1995
© HarperCollins Publishers 1995
PO Box, Glasgow G4 0NB

ISBN 0 00 470902 0

A catalogue record for this book is available
from the British Library.

Typeset by Morton Word Processing Ltd.
Scarborough, England

Printed and bound in Great Britain
by HarperCollins Manufacturing

# Introduction

The *Collins Gem English School Thesaurus* is arranged in a single alphabetical list of main-entry words, like a dictionary. To find exactly the right word for your purpose, look up the word which is your starting point. There, you will find a selection of alternatives which can be used to replace it. If the original word has more than one meaning, the alternative words are grouped in separate numbered lists. In addition, clear definitions of each word and each sense are given, so that the student can be confident of making the right choice. And to help the user even further, an example is given for each sense of each word, showing how it is used. These examples are taken from the Bank of English, an impressive database of over 200 million words of written and spoken English, so that they represent the words as they are really used.

When you are choosing an alternative word from the list given, remember that the context is important. One word may be more appropriate as a substitute for the word you have in mind in one situation, while another is more suitable in a different context. The list of synonyms given for a main entry word or sense may cover several slightly different shades of meaning, so you must think carefully before choosing one as an alternative.

In addition to giving practical everyday help in all contexts and situations where good English is required, the thesaurus, especially when used in conjunction with its companion volume, the *Collins Gem English School Dictionary*, will help you to increase your vocabulary and develop your language skills.

# EDITORIAL STAFF

*Managing Editor*
Marian Makins

*Senior Editor*
**Lorna Knight**

*Lexicographers*
Ian Brookes, Mary O'Neill

*Computing Staff*
Jane Creevy

**Corpus Acknowledgements**
We would like to thank those authors and publishers
who kindly gave permission for copyright material to be
used in the Bank of English. We would also like to thank
Times Newspapers Ltd for providing valuable data.

# *A a*

## abandon

(verb) If you abandon someone or something, you leave them or give them up permanently.

e.g. *Carolyn abandoned her car.*

desert evacuate forsake jilt leave quit vacate

## ability

(noun) Your ability to do something is the quality of intelligence or skill that you have that enables you to do it.

e.g. *the ability to get on with others.*

aptitude capability capacity competence expertise facility faculty flair gift knack power proficiency skill talent

## able

**1.** (adjective) If you are able to do something, you can do it.

e.g. *I may be able to call you later.*

adequate capable fit

**2.** Someone who is able is very clever or talented.

e.g. *Charles is a very able journalist.*

accomplished adept capable clever competent efficient experienced expert gifted masterly practised proficient qualified skilful skilled talented

## abnormality

(noun) An abnormality is something that is not normal or usual.

e.g. *an abnormality in the heart.*

> aberration  deviation  eccentricity  irregularity
> oddity  peculiarity  singularity

## abolish

(verb) To abolish something means to put an end to it officially.

e.g. *a bill to abolish the death penalty.*

> annul  axe  cancel  do away with  eliminate  end
> repeal  revoke  stamp out  suppress  wipe out

## absent

(adjective) Something that is absent is not present in a place or situation.

e.g. *The ambassador planned to be absent from Moscow.*

> away  elsewhere  gone  lacking  missing  out
> wanting

## absorb

(verb) If something absorbs liquid or gas, it soaks it up.

e.g. *Plants absorb carbon dioxide from the air.*

> assimilate  digest  receive  soak up  take in

## abstain

(verb) If you abstain from something, you do not do it or have it.

e.g. *The patients had to abstain from alcohol.*

> avoid  deny yourself  forgo  give up  refrain from
> stop

e.g. *an adequate diet.*

enough  fair  passable  satisfactory  sufficient

## advance

(noun) Advance in something is progress in it.

e.g. *scientific advance.*

development  progress  step forward

## advertise

(verb) If you advertise something, you tell people about it in a newspaper or poster, or on TV.

e.g. *Kasparov is paid a small fortune to advertise drinks.*

announce  plug *slang*  promote  publicize  push *informal*

## advertisement

(noun) An advertisement is an announcement about something in a newspaper or poster, or on TV.

e.g. *an advertisement for a new magazine.*

ad *informal*  advert *informal*  announcement
commercial  notice  plug *slang*  promotion
publicity

## advice

(noun) Advice is an opinion or suggestion from someone about what you should do.

e.g. *He sought my advice as to how a chef should behave.*

counsel  guidance  help  opinion
recommendation  suggestion  view

## advise

(verb) If you advise someone to do something, you tell them that you think they should do it.

e.g. *Steve's mother advised him to cancel his trip.*
counsel  guide  recommend  suggest  urge

## affect

(verb) If something affects you, it influences you or changes you in some way.

e.g. *This experience affected her deeply.*
alter  change  concern  influence

## afraid

(adjective) If you are afraid, you are very frightened.

e.g. *I am afraid of flying.*
alarmed  apprehensive  fearful  frightened
nervous  scared  terrified

## after

**1.** (preposition) later than a particular time, date, or event.

e.g. *I'll come round after dinner.*
following

**2.** (adverb) at a later time.

e.g. *Christopher was taken to hospital but died soon after.*
afterwards  later  subsequently  thereafter

## again

(adverb) returning to the same state or place as before.

e.g. *Her back began to hurt her again.*
afresh  anew  once more

## aggressive

(adjective) full of anger, hostility, and violence.

e.g. *an aggressive crowd.*

> antagonistic belligerent hostile pugnacious quarrelsome truculent

## agonizing or agonising

(adjective) extremely painful, either physically or mentally.

e.g. *an agonizing decision.*

> excruciating painful

## agony

(noun) very great physical or mental pain.

e.g. *He crashed to the ground in agony.*

> anguish distress hell misery pain suffering torment torture

## agree

**1.** (verb) If you agree with someone, you have the same opinion as them.

e.g. *Plenty of experts agree with him.*

> accord concur

**2.** If you agree to do something, you say that you will do it.

e.g. *I agreed to return to London.*

> accede acquiesce assent comply consent

## agreement

**1.** (noun) An agreement is a joint decision that has been reached by two or more people.

e.g. *I signed an agreement with the US Army.*

> arrangement bargain compact contract

covenant  deal  pact  settlement  treaty
understanding

**2.** Two people who are in agreement have the same opinion about something.

e.g. *All were in agreement about the excellent performance.*

accord  accordance  concord  concurrence
harmony

## aim

**1.** (verb) If you aim an object or weapon at someone or something, you point it at them.

e.g. *He aimed the gun at two pupils.*

direct  level  point

**2.** If you aim to do something, you are planning or hoping to do it.

e.g. *We aim to improve standards.*

aspire  intend  mean  plan  propose  seek  want
wish

**3.** If you aim an action at a particular group, you intend them to be influenced by it.

e.g. *an anti-smoking campaign aimed at teenagers.*

direct  level

**4.** (noun) Your aim is what you intend to achieve.

e.g. *My aim is to win a lot more races.*

ambition  aspiration  desire  end  goal  intent
intention  object  objective  purpose  target  wish

## alert

(adjective) paying full attention to what is happening.

e.g. *The criminal was spotted by an alert member of the public.*

> attentive  observant  perceptive  vigilant  watchful wide-awake

## alias

(noun) An alias is a false name used by a criminal.

e.g. *He had been operating under an alias.*

> assumed name  pseudonym

## alive

(adjective) living.

e.g. *Both his parents are still alive.*

> animate  breathing  live  living

## alliance

(noun) An alliance is a group of people, organizations, or countries working together for similar aims.

e.g. *a military alliance.*

> affiliation  association  coalition  confederation federation  league  union

## all right

(adjective) If something is all right, it is satisfactory or acceptable.

e.g. *At first glance, everything looked all right.*

> acceptable  adequate  fair  fine  not bad  okay *informal*

## ally

**1.** (noun) An ally is a person, organization, or
country that helps and supports another.

e.g. *a close ally of the Labour leader.*

> associate  colleague  confederate  friend  helper
> partner

**2.** (verb) If you ally yourself with someone, you agree
to help and support each other.

e.g. *I won't ally myself with other childless women.*

> affiliate  associate

## almost

(adverb) very nearly, but not completely or exactly.

e.g. *Over the past decade their wages have almost
doubled.*

> about  all but  nearly  practically  virtually

## alone

**1.** (adjective) not with other people or things.

e.g. *He just wanted to be alone.*

> apart  isolated  separate  single  single-handed
> solitary  unaccompanied

**2.** (adverb) not with other people or things.

e.g. *She alone believed his story.*

> only  unaccompanied

## aloud

(adverb) When you read or speak aloud, you speak
loudly enough for other people to hear you.

e.g. *Our father read aloud to us after supper.*

> audibly  clearly  distinctly  out loud  plainly

## amaze

(verb) If something amazes you, it surprises you very much.

e.g. *We have been absolutely amazed by their friendliness.*

astonish astound bowl over daze dumbfound flabbergast stagger stun surprise

## amazing

(adjective) very surprising, remarkable, or difficult to believe.

e.g. *an amazing story.*

fabulous incredible unbelievable wonderful

## among or amongst

(preposition) surrounded by.

e.g. *The bike lay among piles of chains and pedals.*

amid amidst between with

## amount

(noun) An amount of something is how much there is of it.

e.g. *a tiny amount of water.*

degree extent measure number quantity volume

## ancestor

(noun) Your ancestors are the members of your family who lived many years ago and from whom you are descended.

e.g. *I'm rather proud of my Russian ancestors.*

forebear forefather predecessor progenitor

## ancestry

(noun) Your ancestry consists of the people from
whom you are descended.

e.g. *a French citizen of Greek ancestry.*

    lineage  pedigree  stock

## anger

**1.** (noun) Anger is the strong feeling that you get
when you feel that someone has behaved in an unfair,
cruel, or insulting way.

e.g. *The crowd went wild with anger.*

    fury  indignation  ire  outrage  rage  spleen
    temper  wrath

**2.** (verb) If something angers you, it makes you feel
angry.

e.g. *This attitude has angered his family.*

    enrage  incense  infuriate  madden  outrage  rile

## angry

(adjective) very cross or annoyed.

e.g. *An angry crowd gathered on the steps.*

    enraged  furious  incensed  indignant  infuriated
    irate  livid  outraged  raging  wrathful

## animal

(noun) An animal is any living being except a plant,
or any mammal except a human being.

e.g. *She kept most of the animals in small cages.*

    beast  brute  creature

## announce

(verb) If you announce something, you tell people about it publicly or officially.

e.g. *The team was announced on Friday morning.*

broadcast declare proclaim publish reveal tell

## annoy

(verb) If someone or something annoys you, they irritate you and make you fairly angry.

e.g. *Elsie was annoyed by Ford's letter.*

aggravate exasperate gall harass hassle irk irritate needle nettle pester plague provoke rile vex

## annul

(verb) If a marriage or contract is annulled, it is declared invalid, so that legally it is considered never to have existed.

e.g. *The marriage was annulled after a legal battle.*

cancel dissolve invalidate nullify repeal rescind revoke

## answer

**1.** (verb) If you answer someone, you reply to them using words or actions or in writing.

e.g. *No one answered him.*

reply respond retort riposte

**2.** (noun) An answer is the reply you give when you answer someone.

e.g. *I knew the answer to that question.*

rejoinder reply response retort riposte

## apathetic

(adjective) not interested in anything.

e.g. *Young people who have never had a job may become depressed and apathetic.*

half-hearted    indifferent    uninterested

## apparent

(adjective) seeming real rather than actually being real.

e.g. *the apparent success of their marriage.*

ostensible    outward    seeming

## appear

**1.** (verb) When something which you could not see appears, it moves (or you move) so that you can see it.

e.g. *Four or five dolphins suddenly appeared.*

come into view    emerge    materialize    show

**2.** When something new appears, it begins to exist.

e.g. *The book first appeared three years ago.*

arise    come into existence    emerge    occur    turn up

## appointment

(noun) An appointment is an arrangement you have with someone to meet or visit them.

e.g. *an appointment with a doctor.*

arrangement    booking    date    engagement
meeting    rendezvous    tryst

## appreciate

(verb) If you appreciate something, you like it because you recognize its good qualities.

e.g. *He appreciates fine wines.*

   esteem  like  prize  regard  respect  value

## approval

(noun) Approval is agreement given to a plan or request.

e.g. *The plan will require approval from the local authority.*

   agreement  assent  authorization  blessing
   consent  endorsement  okay  permission  sanction

## approve

**1.** (verb) If you approve of something, you think that it is right or good.

e.g. *My mother doesn't approve of smoking.*

   acclaim  admire  applaud  commend  esteem
   favour  like  praise  respect

**2.** If someone in a position of authority approves a plan or idea, they formally agree to it.

e.g. *The board of ministers unanimously approved the project.*

   accept  allow  authorize  endorse  pass  permit
   ratify  sanction

## approximate

(adjective) almost accurate or exact.

e.g. *What was the approximate distance between the cars?.*

   close  estimated  near  rough

## area

(noun) An area is a particular part of a place, country, or the world.

e.g. *a built-up area of London.*

district locality neighbourhood part patch
portion region section sector stretch vicinity
zone

## arrest

(verb) If the police arrest someone, they take them
into custody to decide whether to charge them with
an offence.

e.g. *We want the police to arrest the criminals.*

apprehend capture catch detain seize stop
take

## assess

(verb) If you assess something, you consider it
carefully and make a judgment about it.

e.g. *The two of them assessed the challenge.*

appraise evaluate gauge judge size up

## assign

**1.** (verb) To assign something to someone means to
give it to them officially or to make them responsible
for it.

e.g. *He was assigned a cabin in first class.*

allocate allot consign give grant

**2.** If someone is assigned to do something, they are
officially told to do it.

e.g. *Fox had been assigned to do an article on the Lucan
case.*

appoint choose name nominate select

## associate

(verb) If you associate with a group of people, you spend a lot of time with them.

e.g. *He spent a lot of time associating with criminals.*

consort   fraternize   hobnob   mix

## assume

**1.** (verb) If you assume that something is true, you accept that it is true even though you have not thought about it.

e.g. *Patients often assumed I was a doctor.*

accept   believe   expect   fancy   imagine   suppose
surmise   suspect   think

**2.** To assume responsibility for something means to put yourself in charge of it.

e.g. *He assumed command of the navy.*

accept   shoulder   take on   take over   take up
undertake

**3.** If you assume a particular appearance, you start to have it.

e.g. *He assumed an expression of indifference.*

adopt   affect   feign   put on   sham   simulate

## attack

**1.** (verb) To attack someone means to use violence against them so as to hurt or kill them.

e.g. *He was attacked by thugs with metal bats.*

assail   assault   set about   set upon

**2.** (noun) An attack is violent physical action against someone.

e.g. *an appalling and unprovoked attack.*

   assault  offensive  onslaught

**3.** (verb) If you attack someone or their ideas, you criticize them strongly.

e.g. *He attacked the government's economic policies.*

   abuse  blame  censure  criticize  vilify

## attractive

**1.** (adjective) interesting and possibly advantageous.

e.g. *an attractive proposition.*

   agreeable  appealing  interesting  inviting
   tempting

**2.** pleasant to look at or be with.

e.g. *an attractive woman.*

   appealing  beautiful  captivating  charming
   engaging  fetching  gorgeous  handsome  lovely
   pleasing  pretty  winsome

## attribute

(verb) If you attribute something to a circumstance, person, or thing, you believe that it was caused or created by that circumstance, person, or thing.

e.g. *Water pollution was attributed to the use of fertilizers.*

   ascribe  blame  charge  impute

## automatic

(adjective) An automatic machine is programmed to perform tasks without needing a person to operate it.

e.g. *The plane was flying on automatic pilot.*

   mechanical  mechanized

## available

(adjective) Something that is available can be obtained.

e.g. *These products are available in health-food shops.*

accessible  attainable  obtainable

## avant-garde

(adjective) extremely modern or experimental, especially in art, literature, or music.

e.g. *avant-garde jazz.*

experimental  innovative  innovatory  pioneering
progressive

## average

(adjective) Average means standard, normal, or usual.

e.g. *the average American teenager.*

general  normal  ordinary  regular  standard
typical  usual

## avoid

**1.** (verb) If you avoid doing something, you make a deliberate effort not to do it.

e.g. *It is wise to avoid eating fat.*

bypass  circumvent  dodge  evade  shirk  side-step

**2.** If you avoid someone, you keep away from them.

e.g. *He tried to avoid his landlady whenever possible.*

dodge  elude  evade  shun

## aware

(adjective) If you are aware of something, you know about it or realize that it is there.

e.g. *We have to make people aware of the dangers.*

conscious   knowing   mindful

## awful

(adjective) very unpleasant or very bad.

e.g. *He was an awful painter.*

appalling   deplorable   dire   dreadful   fearful
frightful   ghastly   hideous   horrible   nasty
shocking   terrible   unpleasant

## awkward

**1.** (adjective) clumsy and uncomfortable.

e.g. *an awkward, stooping movement.*

clumsy   graceless   ham-fisted   ham-handed
maladroit *formal*   ungainly   ungraceful

**2.** embarrassed, shy, or nervous.

e.g. *She may feel a little awkward with us all at first.*

discomfited   embarrassed   ill at ease   nervous   out
of place   self-conscious   shy

# *B b*

## backbone

**1.** (noun) A backbone is the column of linked bones along the middle of a person's or animal's back.

e.g. *Apply pressure on the middle of the backbone with your fist.*

    spinal column   spine   vertebrae

**2.** Backbone is also strength of character.

e.g. *His trouble was lack of backbone.*

    courage   determination   firmness   fortitude   grit
    mettle   nerve   pluck

## backside

(noun; an informal word) Your backside is the part of your body that you sit on.

e.g. *She slipped and slid downhill on her backside.*

    bottom   posterior   rear   rump

## bad

**1.** (adjective) evil or immoral in character or behaviour.

e.g. *a bad person.*

    corrupt   criminal   delinquent   evil   immoral   mean
    sinful   vile   villainous   wicked

**2.** insufficient or of poor quality.

e.g. *The pay was bad.*

    defective   deficient   faulty   imperfect   inadequate
    incorrect   inferior   poor   unsatisfactory

**3.** Bad food is not suitable for eating, because it has started to decay.

e.g. *a bad egg.*

> decayed  mouldy  off  putrid  rancid  rotten  sour
> substandard  unhealthy

## ball

(noun) A ball is any object shaped like a sphere, especially one used in games such as tennis, cricket, and football.

e.g. *A child threw a ball of newspaper into the road.*

> globe  orb  pellet  sphere

## ban

**1.** (verb) If something is banned, or if you are banned from doing it or using it, you are not allowed to do it or use it.

e.g. *proposals to ban smoking.*

> bar  boycott  debar  forbid  outlaw  prohibit
> proscribe

**2.** (noun) If there is a ban on something, it is not allowed.

e.g. *a ban on fox hunting.*

> embargo  prohibition  proscription  restriction
> suppression

## banish

(verb) To banish someone means to send them into exile.

e.g. *He was banished to Germany.*

> deport  exile  expel  outlaw  transport

## bare

**1.** (adjective) If a part of your body is bare, it is not covered by any clothing.

e.g. *bare legs.*

  exposed naked nude stark stripped uncovered undressed

**2.** If something is bare, it has nothing on top of it or inside it.

e.g. *a small bare office.*

  blank denuded empty poor scanty unfurnished vacant

## barrage

**1.** (noun) A barrage of questions or complaints is a lot of them all coming at the same time.

e.g. *The news was greeted with a barrage of criticism.*

  bombardment onslaught storm volley

**2.** A barrage is continuous artillery fire over a wide area, to prevent the enemy from moving.

e.g. *Police came under a barrage of missiles.*

  battery bombardment fusillade salvo shelling volley

## barren

**1.** (adjective) Barren land has soil of such poor quality that plants cannot grow on it.

e.g. *a barren, waterless desert.*

  arid desolate dry empty infertile unproductive waste

**2.** If a female is barren, she is physically incapable of having offspring.

e.g. *a three-year-old barren mare.*

    childless  infertile  sterile

## barrier

(noun) A barrier is a fence or wall that prevents people or animals getting from one area to another.

e.g. *Jim had climbed over the barrier on to the track.*

    bar  barricade  fence  obstruction  railing

## base

**1.** (noun) The base of something is its lowest part, which often supports the rest.

e.g. *the base of the hill.*

    bed  bottom  foot  foundation  pedestal  rest
    stand  support

**2.** (adjective; a literary use) A base act is one which is shocking and contemptible.

e.g. *He would never suspect her of so base a betrayal.*

    contemptible  despicable  dishonourable  ignoble
    low  mean  shameful

## basic

(adjective) The basic aspects of something are the most necessary ones.

e.g. *the basic necessities of life.*

    central  elementary  essential  fundamental
    intrinsic  key  primary  rudimentary  underlying
    vital

## basis

**1.** (noun) The basis of something is the essential

main principle from which it can be developed.

e.g. *The same colour theme is used as the basis for several patterns.*

  base foundation groundwork

**2.** The basis for a belief is the facts that support it.

e.g. *There is no basis for this assumption.*

  foundation ground support

## bay

(noun) A bay is a part of a coastline where the land curves inwards.

e.g. *We anchored one evening in a deserted bay.*

  cove gulf inlet sound

## beach

(noun) A beach is an area of sand or pebbles beside the sea.

e.g. *The beach stretches along the west coast.*

  coast sands seashore seaside shore strand

## beat

**1.** (verb) To beat someone or something means to hit them hard and repeatedly.

e.g. *He threatened to beat her.*

  batter buffet flog hit lash pound punch
  strike thrash whip

**2.** If you beat someone in a race, game, or competition, you defeat them or do better than them.

e.g. *County beat Brighton 3-1 in the final.*

  conquer defeat lick *informal* outdo overcome
  surpass trounce vanquish

## beautiful

(adjective) very attractive or pleasing.

e.g. *beautiful harmonies.*

appealing  charming  comely  delightful  exquisite
glamorous  gorgeous  handsome  lovely  ravishing
stunning

## before

(adverb) If you have done something before, you have
done it on a previous occasion.

e.g. *Never before had I seen such a moon.*

beforehand  earlier  formerly  previously  sooner

## beg

(verb) When people beg, they ask for food or money,
because they are very poor.

e.g. *She was reduced to begging on the streets.*

beseech  cadge  entreat  implore  importune
plead  pray  solicit

## begin

(verb) If you begin to do something, you start doing
it. When something begins, it starts.

e.g. *I began to walk back to the car.*

commence  initiate  instigate  institute  launch
prepare  set about  start

## beginner

(noun) A beginner is someone who has just started
learning to do something and cannot do it very well
yet.

e.g. *Smaller sails are easier for beginners to handle.*

amateur  apprentice  fledgling  learner  novice

recruit  tyro

## belief

(noun) A belief is one of the principles of a religion or moral system.

e.g. *their belief in equality.*

creed  doctrine  ideology  philosophy  principles
tenet

## belittle

(verb) If you belittle someone or something, you make them seem unimportant.

e.g. *He derided my taste and belittled my opinions.*

decry  denigrate  diminish  disparage

## beloved

(adjective) A beloved person or thing is one that you feel a great affection for.

e.g. *Someone stole my beloved bicycle.*

adored  cherished  darling  dear  dearest  loved
precious  sweet

## bench

(noun) A bench is a long seat that two or more people can sit on.

e.g. *We sat on a concrete bench in the sun.*

form  pew  seat

## bend

**1.** (verb) When you bend something, you use force to make it curved or angular.

e.g. *Most magicians can bend spoons or keys.*

buckle  crook  curve  flex  twist  warp

**2.** When you bend, you move your head and shoulders forwards and downwards.

e.g. *He bent to untie his shoes.*

   lean   stoop

## benefactor

(noun) A benefactor is a person who helps to support a person or institution by giving money.

e.g. *An anonymous benefactor stepped in to provide the prize money.*

   backer   patron   promoter   sponsor

## beneficial

(adjective) Something that is beneficial is good for people.

e.g. *the beneficial effects of exercise.*

   advantageous   favourable   helpful   profitable
   useful   valuable   wholesome

## benefit

**1.** (noun) The benefits of something are the advantages that it brings to people.

e.g. *the benefits of relaxation.*

   advantage   asset   blessing   boon   gain   good
   help   profit

**2.** (verb) If you benefit from something, or if something benefits you, it helps you.

e.g. *The children benefit from having regular playmates.*

   aid   assist   gain   profit

## beside

(preposition) If one thing is beside something else,

they are next to each other.

e.g. *a house beside the sea.*

> adjacent to  alongside  near  neighbouring  next to
> overlooking

# best

(adjective) superior to everything else of its type.

e.g. *the best holiday I ever had.*

> choice  elite  finest  first  first-rate  foremost
> leading  outstanding  perfect  pre-eminent
> superlative  supreme  top

# betray

**1.** (verb) If you betray someone who trusts you, you do something which harms them, such as helping their enemies.

e.g. *This individual was willing to betray his master.*

> abandon  desert  double-cross  forsake  give away
> sell out

**2.** If you betray a secret, you tell it to someone you should not tell it to.

e.g. *He was jailed for betraying top-secret information.*

> disclose  divulge  give away  tell

**3.** If you betray your feelings or thoughts, you show them without intending to.

e.g. *His face betrayed nerves.*

> evince  expose  give away  reveal  show

# better

(adjective) superior to others.

e.g. *much better than expected.*

excelling finer fitter greater preferable superior surpassing worthier

## beware

(verb) If you tell someone to beware of something, you are warning them that it might be dangerous or harmful.

e.g. *Police have warned the public to beware of an escaped prisoner.*

be careful  look out  mind  shun  watch out

## bias

(noun) Someone who shows bias unfairly favours one person or thing.

e.g. *Tests have to be carefully constructed in order to avoid bias.*

bigotry  discrimination  favouritism  leaning partiality  prejudice  slant

## biased

(adjective) favouring one person or thing unfairly.

e.g. *biased attitudes.*

bigoted  one-sided  partial  partisan  predisposed prejudiced  slanted  weighted

## big

(adjective) large in size, extent, or importance.

e.g. *a big house.*

bulky  considerable  eminent  extensive  important large  prodigious  prominent  serious  significant sizeable  spacious  substantial

## bill

(noun) A bill is a written statement of how much is owed for goods or services.

e.g. *We received a telephone bill for forty-four pounds.*

    account  charges  invoice  reckoning

## bit

(noun) A bit of something is a small amount of it.

e.g. *a bit of coal.*

    crumb  fragment  grain  iota  jot  mite  morsel
    part  piece  scrap

## bitter

**1.** (adjective) If someone is bitter, they feel angry and resentful.

e.g. *a bitter and hateful old man.*

    acrimonious  embittered  resentful  sore  sour

**2.** In a bitter argument or war, people argue or fight fiercely and angrily.

e.g. *a bitter power struggle.*

    acrimonious  hostile  rancorous

**3.** Something that tastes bitter has a sharp, unpleasant taste.

e.g. *The coffee was bitter.*

    acid  acrid  astringent  sharp  sour  tart  vinegary

## black

(adjective) A surface that is completely black reflects no light at all.

e.g. *the black night air.*

    dark  dusky  ebony  jet  pitch-black  sable

## blame

**1.** (verb) If someone blames you for something bad that has happened, they believe you caused it or are responsible for it.

e.g. *My father does not blame you for what Arthur did.*

accuse   charge   hold responsible   reproach

**2.** (noun) The blame for something bad is the responsibility for causing it.

e.g. *He had to take the blame for everything.*

culpability   fault   guilt   liability   onus   responsibility

## blank

(adjective) If you look blank, your face shows no feeling, understanding, or interest.

e.g. *blank stares.*

expressionless   impassive   uncomprehending
vacant   vacuous

## blasphemy

(noun) Blasphemy is speech or behaviour that shows disrespect for God or for things people regard as holy.

e.g. *a radio play full of shrieks, obscenities and blasphemies.*

desecration   impiety   profanity   sacrilege

## bless

(verb) When a priest blesses people or things, he asks for God's favour and protection for them.

e.g. *The hospital chaplain said prayers and blessed the ward.*

consecrate   dedicate   sanctify

## blessing

(noun) A blessing is something good that you are thankful for.

e.g. *Good health is the greatest blessing.*

> advantage benefit boon bounty favour gift godsend

## block

**1.** (noun) A block of something is a large rectangular piece of it.

e.g. *a block of marble.*

> bar brick cake chunk cube hunk square

**2.** (verb) To block a road, channel, or pipe means to put something across it so that nothing can get through.

e.g. *The vehicle was blocking a narrow country lane.*

> choke clog close obstruct

**3.** If something blocks your view, it is in the way and prevents you from seeing what you want to see.

e.g. *TV cameras had blocked their view of the show.*

> obstruct

**4.** If someone blocks something, they prevent it from happening.

e.g. *The council blocked his plans.*

> check deter halt hinder impede obstruct stop

## blockage

(noun) When there is a blockage in a pipe, tube, or tunnel, something is clogging it.

e.g. *Our workmen have cleared the blockage and the*

*system is working.*

impediment   obstruction   stoppage

## blunt

(adjective) If you are blunt, you say exactly what you think, without trying to be polite.

e.g. *He is blunt, outspoken, practical, and down to earth.*

abrupt   bluff   brusque   forthright   frank
outspoken   tactless

## blush

(verb) If you blush, your face becomes redder than usual, because you are ashamed or embarrassed.

e.g. *Even to think about it made her blush with shame.*

colour   crimson   flush   redden

## board

(noun) Board is the meals provided when you stay somewhere.

e.g. *The price includes full board.*

food   meals   provisions

## boast

(verb) If you boast about your possessions or achievements, you talk about them proudly, especially to impress other people.

e.g. *I boasted about my holiday in Thailand.*

blow your own trumpet   brag   crow   exaggerate
show off   strut   swagger

## body

(noun) Your body is either all your physical parts or just your trunk, excluding your head and limbs.

e.g. *Her body felt stiff and painful.*

> build figure form frame physique shape torso trunk

## bog

(noun) A bog is an area of land which is wet and permanently spongy.

e.g. *Both waded into the four feet deep bog.*

> fen marsh mire morass quagmire swamp

## boil

(noun) A boil is a red swelling on your skin.

e.g. *Painful boils appeared on my face.*

> carbuncle pustule

## boisterous

(adjective) Someone who is boisterous is noisy, lively, and rather rough.

e.g. *They were a boisterous friendly couple.*

> bouncy noisy riotous rollicking rowdy unruly wild

## bold

**1.** (adjective) confident and not shy or embarrassed.

e.g. *He was not bold enough to ask them.*

> audacious brash brazen dauntless enterprising fearless forward intrepid pert spirited

**2.** clear and noticeable.

e.g. *bold colours.*

> bright colourful conspicuous eye-catching flashy lively loud prominent striking strong vivid

## bomb

(verb) When a place is bombed, it is attacked with bombs.

e.g. *Threats were made to bomb his house.*

blast blitz blow up bombard destroy shell

## bond

**1.** (noun) A bond is a close relationship between people.

e.g. *Females have a wonderful bond with their babies.*

affinity attachment connection link tie

**2.** Bonds are also feelings or obligations that force you to behave in a particular way.

e.g. *the social bonds of community.*

fetter tie

## boring

(adjective) dull and uninteresting.

e.g. *I found staying at home rather boring.*

dull flat humdrum insipid monotonous routine
tedious tiresome tiring wearisome

## bossy

(adjective) A bossy person enjoys telling other people what to do.

e.g. *She remembers being a rather bossy little girl.*

dictatorial domineering high-handed imperious
lordly overbearing tyrannical

## botch

(verb; an informal word) If you botch something, you do it badly or clumsily.

e.g. *She had completely botched one of the tasks.*

bungle mess up mismanage screw up *informal* spoil

# bounce

(verb) When an object bounces, it springs back from something after hitting it. If you bounce an object, such as a ball, you throw it against a surface to make it do this.

e.g. *A wheel flew off the car and bounced over the safety barrier.*

bound rebound recoil ricochet spring

# boy

(noun) A boy is a male child.

e.g. *She gave birth to a healthy baby boy.*

lad stripling youngster youth

# boycott

(verb) If you boycott a person, organization, product, or event, you refuse to have anything to do with it.

e.g. *The opposition is threatening to boycott parliament.*

black blacklist ostracize outlaw proscribe

# brave

(adjective) A brave person is willing to do dangerous things and does not show any fear.

e.g. *an awards ceremony for brave firemen.*

bold courageous daring fearless gallant heroic intrepid plucky valiant

# breach

(noun) A breach of an agreement or law is an action that breaks it.

e.g. _a breach of contract._

contravention infringement transgression
violation

## break

**1.** (verb) When an object breaks, it is damaged and
separates into pieces.

e.g. _A pane of glass broke in the kitchen._

burst crack fracture fragment rupture shatter
smash snap splinter split tear

**2.** If you break a rule, promise, or agreement, you
fail to keep it.

e.g. _Her employers were breaking the law._

breach contravene disregard infringe
transgress violate

## breed

**1.** (verb) When animals breed, they mate and
produce offspring.

e.g. _These birds usually attempt to breed during May to
September._

multiply procreate reproduce

**2.** (noun) A breed of animal is a particular type of it.

e.g. _I like most breeds of dogs._

kind sort species stock strain type variety

## brief

(adjective) Something that is brief lasts only a short
time.

e.g. _They allowed him a brief rest._

cursory fleeting limited little momentary quick

short short-lived swift transitory

## bright

(adjective) strong and startling.

e.g. *a bright light.*

blazing bold brilliant dazzling gleaming
glistening glittering glowing intense luminous
radiant vivid

## broad-minded

(adjective) Someone who is broad-minded is tolerant
of behaviour that other people may find upsetting or
immoral.

e.g. *He knew his uncle to be a broad-minded man.*

indulgent liberal open-minded permissive
tolerant

## broke

(adjective; an informal use) If you are broke, you have
no money.

e.g. *The company was broke.*

bankrupt insolvent penniless

## bug

(noun; an informal use) A bug is a virus or minor
infection.

e.g. *He was recovering from a stomach bug.*

disease germ infection microorganism virus

## build

(verb) To build something such as a house or a
bridge means to make it from its parts.

e.g. *The council decided to build a new civic centre.*

assemble construct erect fabricate form make
put up raise

# bulky

(adjective) large and heavy.

e.g. *a bulky package.*

cumbersome unmanageable unwieldy

# bump

(noun) A bump on a surface is a raised, uneven part.

e.g. *The plane hit a bump on the runway.*

bulge hump lump protuberance swelling

# burden

**1.** (noun) A burden is a heavy load.

e.g. *They carried the heavy burden to the gate.*

encumbrance load weight

**2.** If something is a burden to you, it causes you a
lot of worry or hard work.

e.g. *My shyness was a terrible burden.*

affliction anxiety encumbrance millstone onus
strain stress trial trouble weight worry

# bureaucracy

(noun) Bureaucracy is the complex system of rules
and routine procedures which operate in government
departments.

e.g. *I dislike excessive bureaucracy.*

officialdom red tape

# burly

(adjective) A burly man has a broad body and strong
muscles.

e.g. *burly security guards.*
>beefy big brawny bulky hefty muscular
>powerful stocky strapping strong sturdy

## burn

**1.** (verb) If something is burning, it is on fire.

e.g. *In her hut there was a candle burning.*
>blaze flame flicker glow

**2.** To burn something means to destroy it with fire.

e.g. *He burned the documents and books.*
>char ignite incinerate

## burst

(noun) A burst of something is a short period of it.

e.g. *He had a sudden burst of energy.*
>bout fit outbreak spate spell spurt

## business

(noun) A business is an organization which produces
or sells goods or provides a service.

e.g. *a small travel business.*
>company concern enterprise firm industry
>organization venture

## bustle

(noun) Bustle is busy, noisy activity.

e.g. *the perpetual bustle of the harbour.*
>activity commotion excitement flurry fuss
>hurly-burly hurry rush stir to-do tumult

## busy

(adjective) If you are busy, you are in the middle of
doing something.

e.g. *George was busy preparing lunch.*
employed engaged engrossed occupied slaving
working

## buzz

(noun) A buzz is the sound something makes when it
buzzes.

e.g. *a gentle buzz of conversation.*
drone hum

# C c

## call

**1.** (verb) If someone or something is called by a particular name, that is their name.

e.g. *a man called Jeffrey.*

    christen designate dub entitle label name term

**2.** If someone is called before a court of law, they are ordered to appear there.

e.g. *She was called as a witness in the case.*

    invite summon

## calling

(noun) If you have a calling to a particular job, you have a strong feeling that you should do it.

e.g. *Saint Francis received his calling to repair God's church.*

    mission vocation

## callous

(adjective) cruel and showing no concern for other people's feelings.

e.g. *a callous criminal.*

    cold hardened hardhearted heartless uncaring unfeeling

## calm

**1.** (adjective) Someone who is calm is quiet and does not show any worry or excitement.

e.g. *I am very calm and rarely lose my temper.*

collected composed cool imperturbable placid
quiet relaxed sedate self-possessed serene
tranquil unflappable unruffled

**2.** (noun) Calm is a state of quietness and
peacefulness.

e.g. *He liked the calm of the evening.*

calmness composure peacefulness serenity
stillness tranquillity

**3.** (verb) To calm someone means to make them less
upset or excited.

e.g. *She calmed us all down by reading aloud.*

allay hush lull mollify placate quieten relax
soothe

## campaign

(noun) A campaign is a planned set of actions aimed
at achieving a particular result.

e.g. *a campaign to educate people.*

crusade drive movement push

## cancer

(noun) Cancer is a serious disease in which abnormal
cells in a part of the body increase rapidly, producing
growths.

e.g. *stomach cancer.*

carcinoma tumour

## capitalism

(noun) Capitalism is an economic and political system
where business and industry are owned by private
individuals and not by the state.

e.g. *the West's efforts to transform Russia from communism to capitalism.*

> free enterprise   private enterprise

# captain

(noun) The captain of a ship is the officer in charge of it, especially a naval officer.

e.g. *the First Officer, the second ranking officer after the ship's captain.*

> boss   chief   commander   head   leader   master
> officer   skipper

# care

(verb) If you care for someone, you look after them.

e.g. *Children have to be cared for.*

> look after   nurse   take care of   tend

# careful

(adjective) acting sensibly and with care.

e.g. *Be careful what you say to him.*

> cautious   chary   circumspect   mindful   particular
> prudent   vigilant   wary   watchful

# careless

(adjective) doing something badly without enough attention.

e.g. *careless driving.*

> cavalier   haphazard   incautious   lackadaisical   lax
> neglectful   negligent   offhand   perfunctory
> slapdash   slipshod   sloppy *informal*   thoughtless
> unthinking

## caress

(verb) If you caress someone, you stroke them gently and affectionately.

e.g. *He caressed her hand.*

 fondle stroke

## cargo

(noun) Cargo is the goods carried on a ship or plane.

e.g. *The planes will be used for cargo rather than passenger flights.*

 consignment freight load shipment

## carry

(verb) When a vehicle carries people, they travel in it.

e.g. *The aircraft can carry as many as 39 passengers.*

 bear convey take transport

## carve

(verb) To carve an object means to cut it out of a substance such as stone or wood.

e.g. *ancient Christian dwellings carved from stone.*

 chisel cut engrave hew sculpt whittle

## case

(noun) A case is a particular situation, event, or example.

e.g. *a clear case of mistaken identity.*

 circumstance condition event example
 illustration instance occasion occurrence
 position situation specimen state

## cast

(noun) The cast of a play or film is all the people who act in it.

e.g. *a largely unknown cast.*

actors  characters  company  dramatis personae

## casual

(adjective) careless or without interest.

e.g. *a casual glance over his shoulder.*

blasé  indifferent  nonchalant  offhand
perfunctory  unconcerned

## catch

**1.** (verb) To catch an animal means to stop it from moving freely after chasing or trapping it.

e.g. *He caught three fish in his net.*

bag  capture  ensnare  entrap  snare  trap

**2.** When the police catch criminals, they find them and arrest them.

e.g. *Many offenders are not caught.*

apprehend  arrest  capture  lift *slang*  nail *informal*
seize  take prisoner

**3.** If you catch a cold or a disease, you become infected with it.

e.g. *I've caught that stomach bug that's going round.*

contract  develop  go down with

**4.** (noun) If there is a catch in something, there is a problem or hidden complication.

e.g. *When I said I'd do it, I didn't realise there was a catch.*

disadvantage drawback snag trap trick

## cause

(verb) To cause something means to make it happen.

e.g. *A broken-down lorry is causing a tailback on the motorway.*

bring about create effect engender generate
give rise to lead to occasion precipitate produce

## celebrate

(verb) If you celebrate, or celebrate something, you do something special and enjoyable in honour of it.

e.g. *a party to celebrate the end of the exams.*

exult honour rejoice

## censor

(verb) If someone censors a book or film, they cut or ban parts of it that are considered unsuitable for the public.

e.g. *Some argue that nothing should be censored, however unpleasant.*

bowdlerize cut expurgate

## centralize

(verb) To centralize a system means to bring the organization of it under the control of one central group.

e.g. *a system for centralized record keeping.*

amalgamate concentrate incorporate rationalize
streamline unify

## centre

(noun) The centre of an object or area is the middle of it.

e.g. *a hotel in the centre of town.*
    core   heart   hub   middle

## ceremony

(noun) A ceremony is a set of formal actions performed at a special occasion or important public event.

e.g. *his recent coronation ceremony.*
    ceremonial   rite   ritual   service

## challenge

(verb) If you challenge something, you question whether it is correct or true.

e.g. *Local community groups challenged this argument.*
    contradict   defy   dispute   question

## chance

(noun) Chance is the way things happen unexpectedly without being planned.

e.g. *I only found out by chance.*
    accident   coincidence   destiny   fate   fluke
    fortune   luck   providence

## change

**1.** (noun) A change in something is a difference or alteration.

e.g. *Steven soon noticed a change in Penny's attitude.*
    adjustment   alteration   conversion   difference
    metamorphosis   modification   transformation

**2.** (verb) When something changes or when you change it, it becomes different.

e.g. *My ideas have changed since then.*

adjust alter convert metamorphose modify transform

## changeable

(adjective) likely to change all the time.

e.g. *changeable weather.*

capricious erratic fickle inconsistent mercurial temperamental unpredictable unstable variable volatile

## character

(noun) The character of a person or place is all the qualities which combine to form their personality or atmosphere.

e.g. *His actions are typical of his brave and strong character.*

constitution disposition identity make-up nature personality quality temper temperament type

## characteristic

**1.** (noun) A characteristic is a quality that is typical of a particular person or thing.

e.g. *Silence is the characteristic of the place.*

attribute feature mark peculiarity property quality trait

**2.** (adjective) Characteristic means typical of a particular person or thing.

e.g. *Two things are very characteristic of his driving.*

distinctive distinguishing idiosyncratic individual peculiar representative special specific typical

## charm

(verb) If you charm someone, you use your ability to be attractive and pleasing on them.

e.g. *She charmed audiences as a comic opera singer.*

attract beguile bewitch captivate delight enchant entrance fascinate please

## chase

(verb) If you chase someone or something, you run or go after them in order to catch them or drive them away.

e.g. *a group of children chasing a football.*

follow pursue run after

## chat

**1.** (noun) A chat is a friendly talk with someone, usually about things that are not very important.

e.g. *He invited me into his living room for an informal chat.*

chatter gossip natter talk tête-à-tête

**2.** (verb) When people chat, they talk to each other in a friendly way.

e.g. *They were able to chat in more than one language.*

chatter gossip natter talk

## cheap

(adjective) Something that is cheap costs very little money, and is sometimes of poor quality.

e.g. *a cheap hotel room.*

bargain cut-price economical inexpensive low-cost low-priced reasonable

### cheat

(verb) If someone cheats, they do wrong or unfair things in order to win or get something that they want.

e.g. *We caught him cheating on an exam paper.*

con *informal* deceive defraud double-cross hoodwink swindle

### cheek

(noun) Cheek is speech or behaviour that is rude or disrespectful.

e.g. *He had the cheek to say I should lose some weight.*

disrespect effrontery gall impertinence impudence insolence nerve temerity

### cheer

(verb) If something cheers you, it makes you feel happier.

e.g. *I was cheered by the prospect of being able to help myself.*

brighten buoy up cheer up comfort console gladden hearten uplift

### cheerful

(adjective) happy and in good spirits.

e.g. *I had never seen her so cheerful.*

blithe breezy bright buoyant cheery chirpy gay happy hearty jaunty jocular jolly jovial joyful light-hearted merry sunny

### cherish

1. (verb) If you cherish something, you care deeply about it and want to keep it or look after it lovingly.

e.g. *The previous owners had loved and cherished the house.*

> care for   treasure

**2.** If you cherish a memory or hope, you have it in your mind and care deeply about it.

e.g. *I cherish the good memories I have of him.*

> cultivate  entertain  foster  harbour  hold dear
> nurse  nurture  sustain  treasure

## child

**1.** (noun) A child is a young person who is not yet an adult.

e.g. *She seemed no more than a child to him.*

> baby  infant  juvenile  kid *informal*  minor  nipper
> *informal*  toddler  tot  youngster

**2.** Someone's child is their son or daughter.

e.g. *She took good care of her child.*

> descendant  issue  offspring  progeny

## childish

(adjective) immature and foolish.

e.g. *I don't have time for childish arguments.*

> babyish  immature  infantile  juvenile  puerile

## choice

**1.** (noun) A choice is a range of different things that are available to choose from.

e.g. *a wider choice of treatments.*

> alternative  option  selection  variety

**2.** (adjective) Choice means of very high quality.

e.g. *choice food and drink.*

best  elite  excellent  hand-picked  prize  select
special

## choose

(verb) To choose something means to decide to have
it or do it.

e.g. *He chose to live in England.*

elect  opt for  pick  select  take

## chop

(verb) To chop something means to cut it with quick,
heavy strokes using an axe or a knife.

e.g. *Eric was in the kitchen chopping onions.*

hack  hew  lop

## chronological

(adjective) arranged in the order in which things
happened.

e.g. *Tell me the whole story in chronological order.*

consecutive  historical

## chunk

(noun) A chunk of something solid is a thick piece of
it.

e.g. *a chunk of ice.*

block  hunk  lump  mass  piece  portion  slab
wad

## circulate

(verb) When you circulate something among people,
you pass it round or tell it to all the people.

e.g. *We circulate a regular newsletter.*

broadcast  disseminate  distribute  issue  make

known  promulgate  spread

## city

(noun) A city is a large town where many people live
and work.

e.g. *the shops and markets of the city.*

conurbation  metropolis  town

## claim

(verb) If you claim that something is true or is the
case, you say that it is, although some people may not
believe you.

e.g. *He claims to have lived in the same house all his life.*

allege  assert  hold  insist  maintain  profess
uphold

## class

(noun) A class of people or things is a group of them
of a particular type or quality.

e.g. *the old class of politicians.*

category  group  kind  order  set  sort  type

## clear

(adjective) easy to understand, see, or hear.

e.g. *He made it clear he did not want to talk.*

apparent  certain  coherent  definite  distinct
evident  explicit  lucid  manifest  obvious  patent
plain  positive  pronounced  unambiguous
unequivocal

## clever

(adjective) intelligent and quick to understand things.

e.g. *He was a very clever fellow with a research career.*

astute  brainy _informal_  bright  brilliant  intelligent
quick  sensible  shrewd  smart

## climb

(verb) To climb means to move upwards.

e.g. _She climbed the stairs._

ascend  mount  rise  scale

## clique

(noun) A clique is a small group of people who stick together and do not mix with other people.

e.g. _I don't have a little clique of friends._

circle  coterie  crowd  faction  gang  group  set

## close

(verb) If you close a meeting, conversation, or event, you bring it to an end.

e.g. _the men's road race, which closed the cycling programme._

complete  conclude  end  finish  terminate  wind up

## cloth

(noun) Cloth is fabric made by a process such as weaving.

e.g. _the blue cloth of her jeans._

fabric  material  textiles

## clothe

(verb) To clothe someone means to give them clothes to wear.

e.g. _Relations used to tell my mother how to clothe me._

attire  dress  garb

## clothes

(plural noun) Clothes are the things people wear on their bodies.

e.g. *She wears very smart clothes.*

apparel attire clothing dress garb garments gear *informal* outfit togs *informal*

## cloudy

(adjective) full of clouds.

e.g. *the cloudy sky.*

dark dim dismal dull gloomy leaden overcast

## clown

(noun) You can refer to any funny or silly person as a clown.

e.g. *I can be a clown to make someone feel better.*

buffoon comedian fool jester joker

## club

**1.** (noun) A club is an organization of people with a particular interest, who meet regularly; also the place where they meet.

e.g. *a science club.*

association company fraternity group guild league society

**2.** A club is also a thick, heavy stick used as a weapon.

e.g. *They beat him with a club.*

bat bludgeon cosh *British* cudgel stick truncheon

## clumsy

**1.** (adjective) moving awkwardly and carelessly.

e.g. *He's so clumsy he's forever breaking things.*

> awkward blundering bungling gawky heavy
> inept lumbering maladroit uncoordinated
> ungainly

**2.** said or done without thought or tact.

e.g. *his clumsy attempts to catch her out.*

> awkward blundering bungling gauche inept
> maladroit

## coach

**1.** (verb) If someone coaches you, they teach you and help you to get better at a sport or a subject.

e.g. *Laura had coached Jane in economics.*

> drill instruct prepare teach train tutor

**2.** (noun) Someone's coach is a person who coaches them in a sport or a subject.

e.g. *my tennis coach.*

> instructor teacher trainer tutor

## coax

(verb) If you coax someone to do something, you gently persuade them to do it.

e.g. *We had a hard job coaxing her to come.*

> cajole entice persuade talk into wheedle

## collapse

(verb) If something such as a building collapses, it falls down suddenly. If a person collapses, they fall down suddenly because they are ill.

e.g. *He collapsed with exhaustion.*

    break down  faint  fall  fall down  give way
    subside

## colleague

(noun) A person's colleagues are the people he or she works with.

e.g. *Your colleagues will be concerned about your going to hospital.*

    associate  workmate

## collection

(noun) A collection of things is a group of them acquired over a period of time.

e.g. *a collection of paintings.*

    accumulation  anthology  compilation  group  set

## collision

(noun) A collision occurs when a moving object hits something.

e.g. *a collision between two boats.*

    accident  bump  crash  impact  pile-up  smash

## colloquial

(adjective) Colloquial words and phrases are informal and used especially in conversation.

e.g. *colloquial Scots.*

    conversational  idiomatic  informal  vernacular

## colony

(noun) A colony is a country controlled by a more powerful country.

e.g. *Sri Lanka, a former British colony.*

outpost    province    settlement

## colour

(noun) The colour of something is the appearance
that it has as a result of reflecting light.

e.g. *ribbons of different colours.*

hue    shade    tint

## come

(verb) If a feeling or situation comes from doing
something, it is the result of it.

e.g. *the strength that comes from belonging to a family.*

arise    emanate    emerge    happen    issue    occur
originate    result

## come across

(verb) If you come across something, you find it by
chance.

e.g. *I came across this old photo while I was clearing out
a cupboard.*

chance on    discover    find    stumble on

## comedian

(noun) A comedian is an entertainer whose job is to
make people laugh, especially by telling jokes or funny
stories.

e.g. *the funniest comedian you've ever seen.*

clown    comic    entertainer    humorist    jester    wit

## comfortable

**1.** (adjective) Something that is comfortable makes
you feel relaxed.

e.g. *The kitchen was a homely, comfortable room.*

    cosy  easy  homely  pleasant  relaxing  snug

**2.** You can say that someone is comfortable when they have enough money to live without financial problems.

e.g. *a plan for a comfortable retirement.*

    affluent  prosperous  rich  well-off  well-to-do

## command

(verb) To command someone to do something means to order them to do it.

e.g. *He commanded his troops to attack.*

    bid  charge  direct  enjoin  order

## commandeer

(verb) If soldiers commandeer something, they officially take it so that they can use it.

e.g. *The loads were commandeered by US troops.*

    appropriate  expropriate  requisition  seize

## commemorate

(verb) If you commemorate an event, you do something special to show that you remember it.

e.g. *an exhibition to commemorate the 250th anniversary of the President's birth.*

    celebrate  honour  keep  remember

## comment

(verb) If you comment on something, you make a remark about it.

e.g. *a plan of the essay for my tutor to comment on.*

    mention  note  observe  remark  say

# commit

(verb) To commit a crime or sin means to do it.

e.g. *a woman unlikely to commit murder.*

carry out  do  execute  perform  perpetrate

# common

**1.** (adjective) If something is common knowledge or a common belief, it is widely known or believed.

e.g. *It is common knowledge that swimming is one of the best forms of exercise.*

accepted  general  popular  prevailing  prevalent
universal  widespread

**2.** If you describe someone as common, you mean they do not have good taste or good manners.

e.g. *The visitors were common and vulgar.*

coarse  low  plebeian  vulgar

# common sense

(noun) Your common sense is your natural ability to behave sensibly and make good judgments.

e.g. *He exhibits common sense in many of his views.*

good sense  practicality  prudence  soundness  wit

# communicate

(verb) If you communicate an idea or a feeling to someone, you make them aware of it.

e.g. *The patient is unable to communicate his wishes.*

convey  impart  pass on  transmit

# company

(noun) If you have company, you have a friend or visitor with you.

e.g. *I enjoyed her company.*

companionship  fellowship  society

## comparable

(adjective) If two things are comparable, they are similar in size or quality.

e.g. *He replaced the TV he'd broken with one of comparable value.*

alike  commensurate  corresponding  equal
equivalent  on a par  similar

## compatible

(adjective) If people or things are compatible, they can live, exist, or work together successfully.

e.g. *We like each other and are compatible.*

harmonious  suited  well-matched

## compensate

**1.** (verb) To compensate someone means to give them money to replace something lost, damaged, or destroyed.

e.g. *The cash will be used to compensate accident victims.*

recompense  refund  reimburse  remunerate

**2.** If one thing compensates for another, it cancels out its bad effects.

e.g. *The trip more than compensated for the hardship.*

atone  balance  cancel (out)  counteract  make up
for  offset  redress

## complacent

(adjective) If someone is complacent, they are self-satisfied and unconcerned about a serious situation.

e.g. *We must never be complacent and say we're doing
well enough.*

pleased with yourself  self-satisfied  smug

## complain

(verb) If you complain, you say that you are not
satisfied with something.

e.g. *She was always complaining about one thing or
another.*

carp  grizzle  grouch *informal*  grouse  grumble
lament  moan  whine  whinge *informal*

## complete

**1.** (adjective) to the greatest degree possible.

e.g. *He always makes a complete mess of things.*

absolute  consummate  outright  perfect
thorough  total  utter

**2.** If something is complete, none of it is missing.

e.g. *a complete set of tools.*

entire  full  intact  perfect  unbroken  undivided
whole

## complex

(adjective) Something that is complex has many
different parts and is complicated.

e.g. *a very complex problem.*

circuitous  complicated  convoluted  intricate
involved  tangled  tortuous

## compulsory

(adjective) If something is compulsory, you have to do
it.

e.g. *compulsory redundancies.*

binding forced mandatory obligatory

# conceit

(noun) Conceit is someone's excessive pride in their appearance, abilities, or achievements.

e.g. *Self-confidence is not the same as conceit.*

arrogance bigheadedness *informal* egotism
narcissism pride vanity

# conceited

(adjective) Someone who is conceited is too proud of their appearance, abilities, or achievements.

e.g. *A conceited person boasts about her own achievements.*

arrogant big-headed egotistical narcissistic
proud vain

# concern

(verb) If something concerns you, it is important to you.

e.g. *Your personal problems don't concern me.*

affect be relevant to interest involve pertain to
relate to

# concise

(adjective) giving all the necessary information using the minimum number of words.

e.g. *a concise guide to each area.*

brief compact condensed laconic pithy short
succinct

## condemn

**1.** (verb) If you condemn something, you say it is bad and unacceptable.

e.g. *The ministers condemned the continued fighting.*

censure criticize damn denounce

**2.** If someone is condemned to a punishment, they are given it.

e.g. *The murderer was condemned to death.*

sentence

**3.** If you are condemned to something unpleasant, you must suffer it.

e.g. *many women who are condemned to poverty.*

doom sentence

## condescending

(adjective) If you are condescending, you show by your behaviour that you think you are superior to other people.

e.g. *condescending sneers.*

disdainful lofty patronizing snobbish snooty supercilious superior

## condition

(noun) A condition is a requirement that must be fulfilled for something else to be possible.

e.g. *He had been banned from drinking alcohol as a condition of bail.*

precondition prerequisite provision proviso requirement rider rule stipulation terms

## conference

(noun) A conference is a meeting at which formal discussions take place.

e.g. *a conference on housing.*

> congress convention forum meeting symposium

## confess

(verb) If you confess to something, you admit it.

e.g. *Your son has confessed to his crimes.*

> acknowledge admit come clean *informal* own up

## confession

(noun) If you make a confession, you admit you have done something wrong.

e.g. *a confession of failure.*

> acknowledgment admission

## confidence

(noun) Someone who has confidence is sure of their own abilities, qualities, or ideas.

e.g. *I could speak with confidence.*

> aplomb assurance certainty conviction self-assurance self-possession

## confident

**1.** (adjective) If you are confident about something, you are sure it will happen the way you want it to.

e.g. *They are confident that demand will grow.*

> certain convinced positive satisfied sure

**2.** People who are confident are sure of their own abilities, qualities, or ideas.

e.g. *John sounded powerful and confident.*

assured   self-assured   self-possessed

## confirm

(verb) To confirm something means to say or show that it is true.

e.g. *Police later confirmed that they had received a call.*

authenticate   bear out   corroborate   endorse
ratify   substantiate   validate   verify

## confirmed

(adjective) You use confirmed to describe someone who has a habit, belief, or way of life that is unlikely to change.

e.g. *a confirmed bachelor.*

chronic   habitual   hardened   inveterate   seasoned

## conflict

1. (noun) Conflict is disagreement and argument.

e.g. *conflict between workers and management.*

antagonism   clash   contention   disagreement
discord   dissension   fight   friction   hostility   strife

2. When there is a conflict of ideas or interests, people have different ideas or interests which cannot all be satisfied.

e.g. *a conflict of loyalties.*

clash   difference   opposition   variance

3. (verb) When ideas or interests conflict, they are different and cannot all be satisfied.

e.g. *Fear and curiosity conflicted within me.*

be at variance   clash   collide   differ   disagree

## conform

(verb) If something conforms to a law or to someone's wishes, it is what is required or wanted.

e.g. *His refusal to conform earned him a reputation as a troublemaker.*

comply   fit in with   follow   go along with   obey   yield

## confuse

(verb) To confuse someone means to make them uncertain about what is happening or what to do.

e.g. *The riddle's purpose was to confuse us.*

baffle   bewilder   flummox   fuddle   mystify   perplex   puzzle

## congeal

(verb) When a liquid congeals, it becomes very thick and sticky.

e.g. *The blood had started to congeal.*

clot   coagulate   curdle

## conscience

(noun) Your conscience is the part of your mind that tells you what is right and wrong.

e.g. *Some criminals have a conscience.*

principles   scruples

## conscientious

(adjective) Someone who is conscientious is very careful to do their work properly.

e.g. *a very conscientious student.*

careful   dedicated   diligent   meticulous

painstaking particular punctilious scrupulous thorough

## consider

(verb) To consider something means to think about it carefully.

e.g. _If an offer were made, we would consider it._

contemplate deliberate mull over muse ponder reflect ruminate think about weigh

## consideration

(noun) Consideration is careful thought about something.

e.g. _a decision demanding careful consideration._

contemplation deliberation examination perusal reflection scrutiny study thought

## consist

(verb) What something consists of is its different parts or members.

e.g. _The brain consists of millions of nerve cells._

be composed of be made up of comprise contain

## constant

(adjective) If an amount or level is constant, it stays the same.

e.g. _a constant temperature._

consistent even fixed immutable regular stable steady unchanging uniform

## consult

**1.** (verb) If you consult someone, you ask for their opinion or advice.

e.g. _If you feel pain, consult your doctor._

ask take counsel

**2.** When people consult each other, they exchange ideas and opinions.

e.g. *They consulted with fellow officers.*

ask confer debate take counsel

## consume

(verb) To consume fuel or energy means to use it up.

e.g. *Running consumes a tremendous amount of energy.*

absorb eat up exhaust expend spend use up wear out

## contact

(verb) If you contact someone, you telephone them or write to them.

e.g. *Where can I contact him?.*

get hold of get in touch with reach

## container

(noun) A container is something such as a box or a bottle that you keep things in.

e.g. *a container for water.*

holder receptacle repository vessel

## contest

(noun) A contest is a competition or game.

e.g. *a boxing contest.*

championship competition game match tournament trial

## contestant

(noun) The contestants in a competition are the people taking part in it.

e.g. *contestants on quiz shows.*

> candidate  competitor  contender  entrant
> participant  player

## contingent

(noun) A contingent is a group of people representing
a country or organization.

e.g. *a strong British contingent.*

> body  delegation  deputation  detachment  lobby

## continual

**1.** (adjective) happening all the time without
stopping.

e.g. *continual headaches.*

> constant  continuous  endless  eternal  everlasting
> incessant  interminable  nonstop  perpetual
> persistent  unceasing  unremitting

**2.** happening again and again.

e.g. *the continual snide remarks.*

> constant  continuous  endless  eternal  everlasting
> frequent  incessant  interminable  nonstop
> perpetual  persistent  recurrent  regular  repeated
> unceasing  unremitting

## continuation

**1.** (noun) The continuation of something is the
continuing of it.

e.g. *the continuation of war.*

> perpetuation  prolongation

**2.** Something that is a continuation of an event
follows it and seems like a part of it.

e.g. *a continuation of his earlier music.*

extension  sequel  supplement

## continue

**1.** (verb) If you continue to do something, you keep doing it.

e.g. *Hanley continued to read his book.*

carry on  go on  keep on  persist

**2.** You also say something continues when it starts again after stopping.

e.g. *She continued after a pause.*

carry on  go on  proceed  recommence  resume

## contribute

(verb) If you contribute money, you give it to help to pay for something.

e.g. *He contributes generously to the Conservative Party.*

chip in *informal*  donate  give  subscribe

## control

(verb) If you control yourself, you make yourself behave calmly when you are angry or upset.

e.g. *Unable to control myself, I started shouting.*

check  constrain  contain  curb  hold back restrain

## controversial

(adjective) Something that is controversial causes a lot of discussion and argument, because many people disapprove of it.

e.g. *controversial ideas.*

contentious  outrageous  provocative

## convenient

(adjective) If something is convenient, it is easy to use or it makes something easy to do.

e.g. *a convenient meeting place.*

handy  helpful  labour-saving  opportune
seasonable  suitable  timely  useful  well-timed

## convince

(verb) To convince someone of something means to persuade them that it is true.

e.g. *I convinced him you could be trusted.*

assure  persuade  prove to  satisfy  sway  win over

## convincing

(adjective) Convincing is used to describe things or people that can make you believe something is true.

e.g. *a convincing argument.*

believable  cogent  credible  persuasive  plausible
powerful  telling

## copy

**1.** (noun) A copy is something made to look like something else.

e.g. *a good copy of her signature.*

counterfeit  duplicate  facsimile  forgery  image
imitation  likeness  replica  reproduction

**2.** (verb) If you copy what someone does, you do the same thing.

e.g. *Children learn from copying their parents.*

ape  follow  imitate  mimic

**3.** If you copy something, you make a copy of it.

e.g. *He copied the chart from a book.*

counterfeit   duplicate   photocopy   replicate
reproduce

## corny

(adjective) very obvious or sentimental and not at all
original.

e.g. *corny old love songs.*

banal   hackneyed   old-fashioned   sentimental
stale   trite

## correct

**1.** (adjective) If something is correct, there are no
mistakes in it.

e.g. *The first correct answer we receive will win the prize.*

accurate   exact   faultless   flawless   precise   right
true

**2.** (verb) If you correct something which is wrong,
you make it right.

e.g. *She corrected my grammar.*

adjust   amend   cure   emend   improve   rectify
redress   reform   remedy   right

## corrupt

**1.** (adjective) Corrupt people act dishonestly or
illegally in return for money or power.

e.g. *corrupt ministers.*

bent *slang*   crooked *informal*   dishonest   fraudulent
rotten   shady   unethical   unprincipled
unscrupulous

**2.** (verb) To corrupt someone means to make them
dishonest or immoral.

e.g. *Power has totally corrupted him.*

bribe  debauch  deprave  pervert

## corruption

(noun; a formal use) Corruption is immoral sexual behaviour.

e.g. *a war against corruption and other vices.*

debauchery  decadence  degeneration  depravity
immorality  impurity  perversion  vice  viciousness
wickedness

## count

**1.** (verb) If you count all the things in a group, you add them up to see how many there are.

e.g. *He counted the number of steps.*

calculate  compute  enumerate  number  reckon
tally  tot up

**2.** (noun) A count is a number reached by counting.

e.g. *The final count is going to be high.*

calculation  computation  enumeration  reckoning
score  tally

## countless

(adjective) too many to count.

e.g. *There had been countless demonstrations.*

endless  incalculable  infinite  innumerable  legion
myriad  *literary*  untold

## country

(noun) A country is one of the political areas the world is divided into.

e.g. *the country of New Zealand.*

kingdom land nation realm state

## county

(noun) A county is a region with its own local government.

e.g. *the remote county of Devon.*

province shire

## coup

(noun) When there is a coup, a group of people seize power in a country.

e.g. *A coup almost overthrew the government.*

coup d'état overthrow takeover

## course

(noun) A course is a piece of land where a sport such as golf is played.

e.g. *a motor racing course.*

circuit racecourse track

## cower

(verb) When someone cowers, they crouch or move backwards because they are afraid.

e.g. *Men were cowering behind vehicles.*

cringe crouch quail shrink

## crack

(noun) A crack is a narrow gap.

e.g. *a deep crack in the ceiling.*

breach break chink cleft cranny crevice
fissure fracture gap rift split

## cram

(verb) If you cram people or things into a place, you put more in than there is room for.

e.g. *People were crammed into the flats.*

compress  crowd  force  jam  overcrowd  pack
pack in  press  shove  squeeze  stuff

## craze

(noun) A craze is something that is very popular for a short time.

e.g. *a new fashion craze.*

cult  fad  fashion  mania  trend  vogue

## credible

(adjective) If someone or something is credible, you can believe or trust them.

e.g. *a credible alternative leader.*

believable  conceivable  imaginable  likely
plausible  possible

## creep

(verb) To creep means to move quietly and slowly.

e.g. *I crept back into the kitchen.*

skulk  slink  sneak  steal  tiptoe

## creepy

(adjective; an informal word) strange and frightening.

e.g. *He could not get rid of that creepy feeling.*

eerie  frightening  scary *informal*  sinister  spooky

## crime

(noun) A crime is an action for which you can be punished by law.

e.g. *a serious crime.*

felony misdeed misdemeanour offence
transgression violation wrong wrongdoing

# criminal

(noun) A criminal is someone who has committed a
crime.

e.g. *a very dangerous criminal.*

crook culprit felon offender transgressor
wrongdoer villain

# cripple

(verb) To cripple someone means to injure them
severely so that they can never move properly again.

e.g. *The blast crippled her.*

disable lame maim paralyse

# critical

**1.** (adjective) A critical time is one which is very
important in determining what happens in the future.

e.g. *a critical point in his career.*

crucial decisive momentous pivotal vital

**2.** A critical situation is a very serious one.

e.g. *The economy is in a critical state.*

dangerous grave perilous precarious serious

**3.** If you are critical of something or someone, you
criticize them.

e.g. *His critical attitude puts a lot of people off.*

carping cavilling censorious derogatory
disparaging scathing

## criticize

(verb) If you criticize someone or something, you say what you think is wrong with them.

e.g. *My parents criticized me endlessly.*

censure  condemn  disparage  find fault with
knock *informal*  put down  slag *informal*  slate
*informal*

## cross

**1.** (verb) If you cross something such as a room or a road, you go to the other side of it.

e.g. *He crossed over to the phone.*

bridge  ford  go across  span  traverse

**2.** Lines or roads that cross meet and go across each other.

e.g. *The pipe crossed under the road.*

crisscross  intersect  meet

**3.** (noun) Something that is a cross between two things is neither one thing nor the other, but a mixture of both.

e.g. *a cross between a donkey and a horse.*

blend  combination  crossbreed  hybrid  mixture
mongrel

## crouch

(verb) If you are crouching, you are leaning forward with your legs bent under you.

e.g. *I crouched down behind the chair.*

bend down  huddle  hunch  squat

### crowd

(noun) A crowd is a large group of people gathered together.

e.g. *A crowd gathered outside.*

> bevy flock horde host mob multitude swarm throng

### crucial

(adjective) If something is crucial, it is very important in determining how something else will be in the future.

e.g. *a crucial role to play.*

> central critical decisive pivotal vital

### crude

**1.** (adjective) rough and simple.

e.g. *a crude weapon.*

> clumsy makeshift primitive rough rudimentary simple unrefined

**2.** A crude person speaks or behaves in a rude and offensive way.

e.g. *You can be quite crude at times.*

> boorish coarse crass dirty gross indecent indelicate lewd obscene ribald rough rude smutty tasteless uncouth vulgar

### cruel

(adjective) Cruel people deliberately cause pain or distress to other people or to animals.

e.g. *a cruel husband.*

> brutal callous cold-blooded hard heartless

inhuman inhumane merciless pitiless
remorseless sadistic unkind vicious

## crumple

(verb) To crumple paper or cloth means to squash it
so that it is full of creases and folds.

e.g. *He crumpled up the paper and tossed it away.*

crease crush rumple screw up

## cry

(verb) When you cry, tears appear in your eyes.

e.g. *She was crying so much she could hardly speak.*

bawl blubber snivel sob wail weep

## cunning

**1.** (adjective) Someone who is cunning uses clever
and deceitful methods to get what they want.

e.g. *a cunning lawyer.*

artful canny crafty devious foxy sharp shifty
sly tricky wily

**2.** (noun) Cunning is the ability to get what you
want using clever and deceitful methods.

e.g. *She's got the cunning of a weasel.*

craftiness deviousness guile slyness wiliness

## cure

**1.** (verb) To cure an illness means to end it.

e.g. *a means of curing the common cold.*

heal remedy

**2.** To cure a sick or injured person means to make
them well.

e.g. *He cured me of hepatitis.*

heal mend restore

## curiosity

(noun) A curiosity is something unusual and interesting.

e.g. *This stuffed turtle is a curiosity.*

curio novelty oddity rarity

## curious

(adjective) Someone who is curious wants to know more about something.

e.g. *He is terribly curious about people.*

inquiring inquisitive interested nosey prying

## custom

**1.** (noun) A custom is a traditional activity.

e.g. *an ancient Chinese custom.*

convention practice ritual tradition way

**2.** A custom is also something usually done at a particular time or in particular circumstances by a person or by the people in a society.

e.g. *It was also my custom to do Christmas shows.*

habit manner practice procedure routine way wont

## customer

(noun) A shop's or firm's customers are the people who buy its goods.

e.g. *the customer of a bank.*

buyer client consumer patron purchaser shopper

## cut

**1.** (verb) If you cut something, you use a knife, scissors, or some other sharp tool to mark it, damage it, or remove parts of it.

e.g. *Cut the butter into small pieces.*

    clip  lacerate  nick  score  sever  slash  slice  slit

**2.** If you cut yourself, you injure yourself on a sharp object.

e.g. *I cut my hand.*

    gash  lacerate  nick  slash  slit  wound

**3.** (noun) A cut is an injury caused by a sharp object.

e.g. *The cut was so deep it needed stitches.*

    gash  incision  laceration  nick  slash  slit  wound

# D d

**danger**

(noun) Danger is the possibility that someone may be harmed or killed.

e.g. *There was widespread danger of disease.*

hazard jeopardy menace peril risk threat

**dangerous**

(adjective) able to or likely to cause hurt or harm.

e.g. *a very dangerous situation.*

hazardous menacing perilous risky threatening treacherous unsafe

**dapper**

(adjective) neat and smart in appearance.

e.g. *a dapper fellow in a black velvet jacket.*

natty neat smart spruce spry stylish trim well-groomed

**dark**

(adjective) If it is dark, there is not enough light to see properly.

e.g. *It was very dark in the tunnel.*

cloudy dim dusky gloomy murky overcast shadowy sombre unlit

**dazed**

(adjective) If you are dazed, you are stunned and unable to think clearly.

e.g. *I was too dazed to say or do anything.*

bemused bewildered confused dizzy dopey *informal* fuddled light-headed muddled stunned stupefied

## deadlock

(noun) A deadlock is a situation in which neither side in a dispute is willing to give in.

e.g. *The talks ended in deadlock.*

impasse stalemate

## dear

1. (adjective) much loved.

e.g. *a very dear friend.*

beloved cherished close esteemed intimate precious

2. Something that is dear is very expensive.

e.g. *I can't afford it, it's too dear.*

costly expensive pricey *informal*

## debatable

(adjective) not absolutely certain.

e.g. *The justness of these wars is debatable.*

arguable borderline controversial disputable doubtful dubious questionable uncertain

## decent

(adjective) Decent people are honest and respectable.

e.g. *He seemed to be a decent man.*

decorous nice polite presentable proper respectable seemly

## deceptive

(adjective) likely to make people believe something that is not true.

e.g. *Appearances can be deceptive.*

ambiguous  deceitful  false  illusory  misleading
mock

## decide

**1.** (verb) If you decide to do something, you choose to do it.

e.g. *I decided to stay on and fight.*

choose  determine  elect  resolve

**2.** If an event or fact decides a situation, it makes a particular result or choice absolutely certain.

e.g. *The cup final was decided on penalties.*

adjudicate  conclude  end  settle

## decision

(noun) A decision is a choice or judgment that is made about something.

e.g. *The editor's decision is final.*

conclusion  judgment  resolution  ruling
settlement  verdict

## declaration

(noun) A declaration is a firm, forceful statement, often an official announcement.

e.g. *a declaration of war.*

affirmation  announcement  assertion
promulgation  pronouncement  statement

## declare

(verb) If you declare something, you say it firmly and forcefully.

e.g *He declared he was going to be famous.*

> affirm announce assert aver avow claim
> maintain proclaim pronounce state

## decorate

(verb) If you decorate something, you make it more attractive by adding some ornament or colour to it.

e.g. *Antonia decorated the cake with cream.*

> adorn beautify deck embellish festoon garnish
> ornament trim

## dedicate

(verb) If you dedicate yourself to something, you devote your time and energy to it.

e.g. *He dedicates himself to golf.*

> commit devote pledge surrender

## deduce

(verb) If you deduce something, you work it out from other facts that you know are true.

e.g. *He deduced that there had been an argument.*

> conclude gather infer reason surmise
> understand

## defile

(verb) To defile something precious or holy means to spoil or damage it.

e.g. *The graves were defiled by vandals.*

> desecrate profane

## deform

(verb) To deform something means to put it out of shape or spoil its appearance.

e.g. *Badly fitting shoes can deform the feet.*

cripple disfigure distort maim twist warp

## defy

(verb) If you defy a person or a law, you openly resist and refuse to obey.

e.g. *He defied doctor's orders.*

challenge confront dare flout scorn slight

## degrade

(verb) If something degrades people, it humiliates or corrupts them.

e.g. *My grandfather always said that work degraded men.*

corrupt debase demean discredit disgrace
pervert shame

## dejected

(adjective) miserable and unhappy.

e.g. *Dejected prisoners sat in rows.*

crestfallen depressed despondent disconsolate
disheartened downcast gloomy morose sad
wretched

## delay

(verb) If you delay doing something, you put it off until a later time.

e.g. *I delayed my decision.*

defer postpone procrastinate put off suspend
temporize

## delete

(verb) To delete something written means to rub it out or remove it.

e.g. *I got permission to delete the whole entry.*

cancel  cross out  erase  expunge  obliterate
remove  rub out

## deliberate

(adjective) intentional or planned in advance.

e.g. *It was a deliberate insult.*

calculated  conscious  considered  intentional
knowing  planned  premeditated  studied  wilful

## delicious

(adjective) very pleasing, especially to taste.

e.g. *delicious fruit.*

appetizing  choice  delectable  luscious
mouthwatering  savoury  scrumptious  tasty

## demanding

(adjective) requiring a lot of time, energy, or attention.

e.g. *He has a demanding job.*

challenging  difficult  exacting  taxing  tough

## demonstrative

(adjective) People who are demonstrative openly show or express their feelings.

e.g. *They are unusually demonstrative and affectionate with their friends.*

effusive  gushing  unreserved

## deny

(verb) If you deny something that has been said, you state that it is untrue.

e.g. *Powell denied reports that he had threatened to resign.*

contradict  gainsay  repudiate

## depend

(verb) If you depend on someone or something, you trust them and rely on them.

e.g. *You can depend on me.*

bank on  count on  rely on  trust

## dependable

(adjective) reliable and trustworthy.

e.g. *He was dependable and loyal.*

faithful  reliable  staunch  steady  sure
trustworthy  trusty  unfailing

## dependent

(adjective) reliant on someone or something.

e.g. *Many countries are almost entirely dependent on tourism.*

conditional  contingent on  helpless  provisional
reliant  subject to  vulnerable

## depressed

(adjective) unhappy and gloomy.

e.g. *I have been feeling depressed about work.*

despondent  dispirited  doleful  down  downcast
fed up *informal*  glum  low  melancholy  sad
unhappy

## deserve

(verb) If you deserve something, you are entitled to it or earn it because of your qualities, achievements, or actions.

e.g. *He deserved a rest.*

  earn  justify  merit  rate  warrant

## deserving

(adjective) worthy of being helped, rewarded, or praised.

e.g. *a deserving charity.*

  commendable  meritorious  praiseworthy  worthy

## desire

**1.** (verb) If you desire something, you want it very much.

e.g. *I desired to expand the business.*

  covet  crave  fancy  hanker after  want  wish

**2.** (noun) A desire is a strong feeling of wanting something.

e.g. *a desire to be rich.*

  appetite  craving  hankering  longing  lust  need
  thirst  want

## despair

(noun) Despair is a total loss of hope.

e.g. *He felt a sense of despair at his own stupidity.*

  anguish  desperation  hopelessness

## despite

(preposition) in spite of.

e.g. *He fell asleep despite all the coffee he'd drunk.*

ascertain check detect discover find out learn verify work out

## determined

(adjective) firmly decided.

e.g. *She was determined not to repeat her error.*

adamant dogged firm intent on resolute single-minded steadfast tenacious

## dictator

(noun) A dictator is a ruler who has complete power in a country, especially one who has taken power by force.

e.g. *the grim rule of the ruthless dictator.*

autocrat despot oppressor tyrant

## diction

(noun) Someone's diction is the clarity with which they speak or sing.

e.g. *a quiet, even-toned voice with perfect diction.*

articulation delivery enunciation intonation pronunciation speech

## die

(verb) When people, animals, or plants die, they stop living.

e.g. *Sir Malcolm died in 1948.*

disappear expire pass away perish vanish

## difference

(noun) The difference between things is the way in which they are unlike each other.

e.g. *the difference between butter and margarine.*

contrast discrepancy disparity dissimilarity
distinction divergence variation

## different

1. (adjective) unlike something else.

e.g. *France is very different from England.*
   contrasting disparate dissimilar divergent unlike

2. distinct and separate, although of the same kind.

e.g. *The lunch supports different charities each year.*
   alternative assorted diverse sundry variant
   varied various

## difficult

1. (adjective) not easy to do, understand, or solve.

e.g. *He was doing a difficult job.*
   demanding formidable hard knotty laborious
   onerous thorny tricky uphill

2. hard to deal with or troublesome, especially
because of being unreasonable or unpredictable.

e.g. *a difficult child.*
   awkward fractious perverse tiresome
   troublesome trying unmanageable

## difficulty

(noun) A difficulty is a problem.

e.g. *If Mr. Dayton were in some kind of difficulty, who
else might he phone?.*
   fix *informal* jam *informal* mess pickle *informal*
   plight predicament spot *informal* trouble

## dilapidated

(adjective) falling to pieces and generally in a bad condition.

e.g. *They had renovated the house from a very dilapidated condition.*

broken down  decayed  decaying  decrepit
neglected  ramshackle  rickety  run down

## diligent

(adjective) hard-working, and showing care and perseverance.

e.g. *a diligent student.*

assiduous  conscientious  indefatigable
industrious  studious  tireless

## direct

(adjective) straightforward, and without delay or evasion.

e.g. *his direct and abrupt manner.*

candid  forthright  frank  matter-of-fact
outspoken  straight  straightforward

## dirt

(noun) Dirt is any unclean substance, such as dust, mud, or stains.

e.g. *His face was streaked with dirt.*

filth  grime  impurity  muck  squalor

## dirty

(adjective) marked or covered with dirt.

e.g. *dirty clothes.*

filthy  foul  grimy  grotty *slang*  grubby  messy
mucky  polluted  soiled

## disadvantage

(noun) A disadvantage is an unfavourable or harmful circumstance.

e.g. *the double disadvantage of being deaf and dumb.*

detriment drawback handicap hindrance
liability minus

## disagree

(verb) If you disagree with someone, you have a different view or opinion from theirs.

e.g. *Lord Morton disagreed with Lord Prosser.*

argue bicker clash differ dissent diverge
quarrel wrangle

## disappear

(verb) To disappear means to stop existing or happening.

e.g. *The pain has disappeared.*

cease dissolve end evaporate fade melt away
pass away vanish wane

## disaster

**1.** (noun) A disaster is an event or accident that causes great distress or destruction.

e.g. *a major rail disaster.*

accident blow calamity cataclysm catastrophe
misfortune tragedy

**2.** A disaster is also a complete failure.

e.g. *The family holiday in Majorca was a disaster.*

catastrophe debacle fiasco

## discard

(verb) To discard something means to get rid of it, because you no longer want it or find it useful.

e.g. *Scoop out the seeds and discard them.*

abandon dispose of ditch *slang* drop dump *informal* jettison scrap shed

## discerning

(adjective) having good taste and judgment.

e.g. *a discerning collector.*

discriminating judicious perceptive perspicacious selective shrewd

## discourage

(verb) To discourage someone means to take away their enthusiasm or confidence to do something.

e.g. *Uncle Alfred discouraged me from writing poetry.*

dampen dash daunt demoralize deter dishearten dismay intimidate

## discussion

(noun) A discussion is a conversation or piece of writing in which a subject is considered in detail, from several points of view.

e.g. *a discussion about football.*

consultation debate dialogue discourse exchange

## disgrace

**1.** (noun) Disgrace is loss of approval and respect by people towards another person.

e.g. *She had brought disgrace to her family.*

discredit disfavour dishonour disrepute

humiliation ignominy infamy opprobrium shame stigma

**2.** (verb) If you disgrace yourself or disgrace someone else, you cause yourself or them to be strongly disapproved of by other people.

e.g. *scenes that have disgraced the game of cricket.*

discredit dishonour humiliate shame

## disgraceful

(adjective) If something is disgraceful, people disapprove of it strongly and think that those who are responsible for it should be ashamed.

e.g. *I complained about his disgraceful behaviour.*

contemptible discreditable dishonourable disreputable infamous outrageous reprehensible scandalous shameful shocking

## disgust

**1.** (noun) Disgust is the feeling aroused in you by something that is morally wrong, shameful, or very unpleasant.

e.g. *The book left her with a strong feeling of disgust.*

abhorrence antipathy detestation distaste loathing repugnance repulsion revulsion

**2.** (verb) To disgust someone means to make them feel sickened and disapproving.

e.g. *The idea disgusted me.*

displease nauseate offend outrage put off repel revolt sicken

## disgusting

(adjective) very unpleasant and offensive.

e.g. *The food was disgusting.*

abominable  foul  gross  hateful  loathsome  nasty
nauseating  odious  offensive  repellent
repugnant  repulsive  revolting  sickening  vile

## dislike

(noun) Dislike is a feeling that you have when you do
not like someone or something.

e.g. *his dislike of men with beards.*

animosity  antagonism  antipathy  aversion
detestation  disapproval  disgust  distaste  enmity
hatred  hostility  loathing  repugnance

## disorder

(noun) Disorder is a lack of organization.

e.g. *The men fled in disorder.*

bedlam  chaos  confusion  disorganization
mayhem  shambles  turmoil

## distant

(adjective) Someone who is distant is cold and
unfriendly.

e.g. *He adopted a very distant attitude.*

aloof  cold  cool  formal  haughty  reserved
standoffish  stiff  unapproachable  withdrawn

## distasteful

(adjective) If you find something distasteful, you think
it is unpleasant or offensive.

e.g. *I find her gossip distasteful.*

abhorrent  disagreeable  displeasing  obnoxious

offensive repugnant repulsive unpalatable
unpleasant unsavoury

## distract

(verb) If something distracts you, your attention is
taken away from what you are doing.

e.g. *A disturbance in the street distracted my attention.*
divert sidetrack

## distress

**1.** (noun) Distress is great suffering.

e.g. *He was in a state of extreme distress when she left him.*

affliction agony anguish anxiety desolation
discomfort grief heartache misery pain
sadness sorrow torment

**2.** (verb) To distress someone means to make them
feel alarmed or unhappy.

e.g. *Her death had profoundly distressed me.*

afflict disturb grieve harrow pain sadden
upset worry wound

## distressing

(adjective) very worrying or upsetting.

e.g. *a distressing new report.*

affecting disturbing harrowing heart-rending
painful sad upsetting

## distribute

(verb) To distribute something means to divide it and
share it out among a number of people.

e.g. *Organisers plan to distribute posters and leaflets.*

assign dispense divide dole out give out share
out

## disturb

(verb) If something disturbs you, it makes you feel
upset or worried.

e.g. *The atmosphere disturbed her.*

agitate alarm disconcert distress fluster
perturb ruffle shake trouble unnerve unsettle
upset worry

## dive

(verb) If an aircraft or bird dives, it flies in a steep
downward path, or drops sharply.

e.g. *His plane stalled and dived into the ground.*

dip plummet plunge swoop

## dizzy

(adjective) having or causing a whirling sensation.

e.g. *He felt sick and dizzy and then passed out.*

dazed faint giddy light-headed reeling shaky
staggering swimming wobbly

## do

(verb) If someone does a task, chore, or activity, they
perform it and finish it.

e.g. *He just didn't want to do any work.*

accomplish achieve carry out complete
conclude discharge effect execute perform

## doubt

(noun) Doubt is a feeling of uncertainty about
whether something is true or possible.

e.g. *There was some doubt about whether the pistol was*

*loaded.*

> disquiet distrust dubiety fear misgiving
> mistrust qualm reservation scepticism suspicion
> uncertainty

# downpour

(noun) A downpour is a heavy fall of rain.

e.g. *Banana plantations were drenched by the downpour.*

> cloudburst deluge flood inundation

# drab

(adjective) dull and unattractive.

e.g. *a drab grey suit.*

> colourless dingy dismal dreary dull flat
> lacklustre sombre

# drag

(verb) If you drag a heavy object somewhere, you pull
it slowly and with difficulty.

e.g. *Four men dragged the driver from his cab.*

> draw haul lug pull tow trail tug yank

# drastic

(adjective) A drastic course of action is very strong
and severe and is usually taken urgently.

e.g. *drastic measures to cut unemployment.*

> desperate dramatic extreme harsh radical
> severe strong

# dreadful

(adjective) very bad or unpleasant.

e.g. *She had dreadful nightmares.*

> abominable abysmal appalling atrocious

deplorable  frightful  ghastly  hideous  horrible
monstrous  shocking  terrible

## drink

**1.** (verb) When you drink, you take liquid into your
mouth and swallow it.

e.g. *You should drink plenty of water.*

drain  gulp  imbibe  sip  swallow  swig *informal*

**2.** To drink also means to drink alcohol.

e.g. *He drinks little and eats carefully.*

booze *informal*  imbibe  tipple

## drudgery

(noun) Drudgery is hard uninteresting work.

e.g. *I hate the drudgery of paperwork.*

chore  donkey-work  grind  labour  slavery  slog
*informal*  toil

## drunk

(adjective) If someone is drunk, they have drunk so
much alcohol that they cannot speak clearly or behave
sensibly.

e.g. *His son was killed by a drunk driver.*

drunken  fuddled  inebriated  intoxicated  merry
*informal*  sloshed *slang*  tight *informal*  tipsy

## dry

(adjective) Something that is dry contains or uses no
water or liquid.

e.g. *a dry cloth.*

arid  barren  dehydrated  parched  thirsty

## dubious

(adjective) not entirely honest, safe, or reliable.

e.g. *dubious sales techniques.*

dodgy *informal* doubtful questionable suspect suspicious

## dull

**1.** (adjective) not at all interesting.

e.g. *She thought the book dull and unoriginal.*

boring commonplace dreary dry flat plain prosaic tedious

**2.** A dull day or a dull sky is very cloudy.

e.g. *The weather was generally dull and rainy.*

cloudy gloomy heavy leaden overcast

## dumb

(adjective) unable to speak.

e.g. *I was dumb with shyness and awe.*

mute silent soundless speechless

## duty

(noun) Duties are things you ought to do or feel you should do, because it is your responsibility to do them.

e.g. *We have a duty as adults to listen to children.*

function obligation responsibility role task

# *E e*

## early

**1.** (adverb) before the arranged or expected time.

e.g. *They arrived early.*

  ahead of time  prematurely  too soon

**2.** (adjective) happening before the arranged or expected time.

e.g. *We had an early dinner.*

  premature  untimely

## earn

(verb) If you earn money, you get it in return for work that you do.

e.g. *As a top model Clare earned a fortune.*

  bring in  gain  get  gross  make  obtain  receive

## ease

**1.** (noun) Ease is lack of difficulty, worry, or hardship.

e.g. *He had sailed through life with relative ease.*

  comfort  contentment  easiness  enjoyment
  facility  leisure

**2.** (verb) When something eases, or when you ease it, it becomes less.

e.g. *She took an aspirin to ease her headache.*

  abate  alleviate  assuage  lessen  lighten
  moderate  relieve

## easy

(adjective) able to be done without difficulty.

e.g. *This book is short and easy to read.*

effortless  light  simple  straightforward
undemanding

## easy-going

(adjective) not easily annoyed or worried.

e.g. *He had a reputation as an easy-going boss.*

calm  laid-back *informal*  placid  relaxed  tolerant

## eccentric

**1.** (adjective) having habits or opinions which other
people think are odd or peculiar.

e.g. *an eccentric professor.*

bizarre  cranky  odd  outlandish  peculiar  queer
quirky  strange  unconventional  weird

**2.** (noun) An eccentric is someone who is eccentric.

e.g. *Artists are notorious eccentrics.*

crank  oddball *informal*  weirdo *informal*

## economy

(noun) Economy is the careful use of things to save
money, time, or energy.

e.g. *For economy, steel tables are used on cheaper models.*

frugality  husbandry  saving  thrift

## ecstasy

(noun) Ecstasy is a feeling of extreme happiness.

e.g. *He jumped up and down in ecstasy.*

bliss  delight  elation  euphoria  exaltation  joy
rapture

## edge

(noun) The edge of something is a border or line where it ends or meets something else.

e.g. *a motel on the edge of a lake.*

border  boundary  brink  fringe  limit  margin
perimeter  rim  side

## efficient

(adjective) capable of doing something well without wasting time or energy.

e.g. *an efficient secretary.*

able  adept  businesslike  capable  competent
proficient  skilful  well-organized  workmanlike

## effort

(noun) Effort is the physical or mental energy needed to do something.

e.g. *Her face screwed up with effort.*

energy  exertion  labour  pains  striving  toil
trouble  work

## eject

(verb) If you eject something or someone, you forcefully push or send them out.

e.g. *The pod was ejected from the spacecraft.*

discharge  emit  expel  throw out

## elaborate

1. (adjective) highly decorated and complicated.

e.g. *elaborate designs.*

complex  complicated  decorated  detailed  fussy
intricate  ornamented  ornate

**2.** (verb) If you elaborate on something, you add more information or detail about it.

e.g. *Dr Bing would not elaborate on the events.*

    add detail  amplify  embellish  expand

## embarrass

(verb) If you embarrass someone, you make them feel shy, ashamed, or uncomfortable.

e.g. *He had never sought to embarrass her by referring to the incident.*

    discomfit  disconcert  humiliate  mortify  shame  show up *informal*

## emergency

(noun) An emergency is an unexpected and serious event which needs immediate action to deal with it.

e.g. *I had a friend nearby who could help out in an emergency.*

    crisis  difficulty  exigency  extremity  necessity  plight  predicament

## emit

(verb) To emit something means to give it out or release it.

e.g. *The food emitted a strong smell.*

    discharge  emanate  exude  give off  give out  issue

## employ

(verb) If you employ someone, you pay them to work for you.

e.g. *The company employs eighteen staff.*

    engage  enlist  hire  take on

## empty

**1.** (adjective) having nothing or nobody inside.

e.g. *an empty house.*

> bare blank hollow unfurnished uninhabited unoccupied vacant void

**2.** without purpose, value, or meaning.

e.g. *empty gestures.*

> aimless hollow meaningless worthless

**3.** (verb) If you empty something, or empty its contents, you remove the contents.

e.g. *I emptied my kitchen cupboards.*

> clear vacate void

## encourage

(verb) If you encourage someone, you give them courage and confidence to do something.

e.g. *Naomi encouraged her to train as a nurse.*

> buoy up egg on embolden incite inspire urge

## end

(noun) The end of something is the farthest point of it.

e.g. *the room at the end of the passage.*

> boundary edge extremity limit tip

## endanger

(verb) To endanger something means to cause it to be in a dangerous and harmful situation.

e.g. *Insecticides can endanger wildlife.*

> imperil jeopardize put at risk threaten

## enemy

(noun) An enemy is a person or group that is hostile or opposed to another person or group.

e.g. *He had many enemies in London.*

    adversary  antagonist  foe  opponent

## energetic

(adjective) having or showing energy or enthusiasm.

e.g. *thousands of energetic volunteers.*

    active  alive  brisk  dynamic  lively  spirited
    tireless  vigorous

## energy

(noun) Energy is the physical strength to do active things.

e.g. *Bill is a man with boundless energy and enthusiasm.*

    drive  force  go  *informal*  power  stamina
    strength  verve  vigour

## engross

(verb) If something or someone engrosses you, they hold all your attention.

e.g. *She was engrossed in her book.*

    absorb  immerse  involve

## entertain

(verb) If you entertain people, you keep them amused, interested, or attentive.

e.g. *He entertained us with wonderful stories.*

    amuse  divert  occupy

## enthusiasm

(noun) Enthusiasm is interest, eagerness, or delight in something that you enjoy.

e.g. *a passionate enthusiasm for sport.*

> ardour  eagerness  fervour  gusto  interest
> keenness  passion  relish  zeal  zest

## entrance

(verb) If something entrances you, it gives you a feeling of wonder and delight.

e.g. *He was immediately entranced by her voice.*

> captivate  charm  enchant  enthral  fascinate

## entry

**1.** (noun) Entry is the act of entering a place.

e.g. *The thieves gained entry by smashing the window.*

> access  admission  admittance  entrance

**2.** An entry is also any place through which you enter somewhere.

e.g. *the entry to the main room.*

> door  doorway  entrance  gate  way in

## equal

(verb) If one thing equals another, it is as good or remarkable as the other.

e.g. *Nobody can equal her skill at the piano.*

> match  parallel  rival

## equality

(noun) Equality is the same status, rights, and responsibilities for all members of a society.

e.g. *There should be equality of opportunity for all.*

equivalence fairness parity

## equip

(verb) If a person or thing is equipped with something, they have it or are provided with it.

e.g. *We were well equipped for the journey.*

fit out furnish kit out provide stock supply

## equipment

(noun) Equipment is all the things that are needed or used for a particular job or activity.

e.g. *photographic equipment.*

accoutrements apparatus gear kit paraphernalia stuff tackle

## equivalent

(noun) An equivalent is something that has the same use, size, value, or effect as something else.

e.g. *Lieutenant Commander is the Navy equivalent to an Army Major.*

counterpart equal match parallel

## era

(noun) An era is a period of time distinguished by a particular feature.

e.g. *the jazz era of the '20s.*

age epoch period time

## erect

(adjective) in a straight and upright position.

e.g. *The hairs stand erect to retain more body heat.*

standing straight upright vertical

## err

(verb) If you err, you make a mistake.

e.g. *To err is human.*

    blunder  miscalculate  slip up

## essence

(noun) The essence of something is the perfect form of it.

e.g. *the essence of a British summer.*

    quintessence  soul  spirit

## establish

(verb) To establish something means to create it or set it up in a permanent way.

e.g. *He has established a successful business.*

    create  found  institute  set up  start

## eternal

(adjective) lasting forever, or seeming to last forever.

e.g. *his eternal complaints.*

    abiding  constant  endless  everlasting  perpetual unending

## etiquette

(noun) Etiquette is a set of rules for behaviour in a particular social situation.

e.g. *a strict observance of army etiquette.*

    code  customs  decorum  formalities  manners propriety  protocol

## even

**1.** (adjective) flat and level.

e.g. *an even layer of chocolate.*

    flat  horizontal  level  smooth  straight

**2.** Scores that are even are exactly the same.

e.g. *Honours were even.*

    equal  fifty-fifty *informal*  level

## event

(noun) An event is something that happens, especially when it is unusual or important.

e.g. *The last great social event of the season.*

    affair  business  episode  happening  incident occasion  occurrence

## everywhere

(adverb) in all places or to all places.

e.g. *Insects were everywhere.*

    all around  all over  omnipresent  ubiquitous

## evict

(verb) To evict someone means to officially force them to leave a place they are occupying.

e.g. *She was to be evicted from her own home.*

    eject  expel  kick out  oust  put out  remove throw out  turf out *informal*

## exaggerate

(verb) To exaggerate something means to make it more noticeable than usual.

e.g. *His Irish brogue was exaggerated for the benefit of the joke he was telling.*

    emphasize  inflate  magnify  overdo overemphasize

## examine

(verb) If you examine something, you inspect it very carefully.

e.g. *Police examined hospital records.*

analyse  inspect  investigate  look over  peruse
scan  scrutinize  study  survey

## example

(noun) An example is something which represents or is typical of a group or set.

e.g. *some examples of early Spanish music.*

illustration  instance  sample  specimen

## excellent

(adjective) very good indeed.

e.g. *We enjoyed an excellent meal.*

admirable  choice  fine  first-rate  great  masterly
outstanding  prime  splendid  superb  superior
superlative

## excessive

(adjective) too great in amount or degree.

e.g. *using excessive force.*

extreme  immoderate  inordinate  overdone
overmuch  undue

## excite

(verb) If somebody or something excites you, they make you feel very happy and nervous or very interested and enthusiastic.

e.g. *I only take on work that excites me.*

electrify  exhilarate  inspire  move  rouse
stimulate  thrill

## exclusive

(adjective) available to or for the use of a small group of rich or privileged people.

e.g. *an exclusive club.*

confined limited private restricted select

## exempt

(verb) To exempt someone from a rule, duty, or obligation means to excuse them from it.

e.g. *Because of his wounded hand he was exempted from hard labour.*

absolve except excuse free let off release relieve

## exercise

(verb) If you exercise your authority, rights, or responsibilities, you use them.

e.g. *I would like to exercise my right to reply.*

apply employ exert practise use utilize wield

## exhaust

(verb) To exhaust someone means to make them so tired that they have no energy left.

e.g. *He was visibly exhausted by the extreme heat.*

debilitate drain enervate fatigue sap tire tire out weaken wear out weary

## expand

(verb) If you expand on or expand upon something, you give more details about it.

e.g. *Claire is keen to expand on the subject.*

amplify elaborate embellish enlarge on expatiate

## expanse

(noun) An expanse is a very large or widespread area.

e.g. *an expanse of sand and desert.*

    area  space  stretch  sweep  tract

## expect

(verb) If you expect something, you believe that it is going to happen or arrive.

e.g. *Shareholders can expect a small profit.*

    anticipate  assume  await  bargain for  foresee
    hope for  look forward to

## expense

(noun) Expense is the money that something costs.

e.g. *the expense of buying electronic instruments.*

    charge  cost  expenditure  outgoings  outlay

## experience

(verb) If you experience a situation or feeling, it happens to you or you are affected by it.

e.g. *She experienced a growing sense of excitement.*

    encounter  feel  go through  have  know  meet
    undergo

## experienced

(adjective) skilled or knowledgeable through doing something for a long time.

e.g. *an experienced sailor.*

    accomplished  knowledgeable  practised  seasoned

## expert

(noun) An expert is someone who is very skilled at

doing something or very knowledgeable about a particular subject.

e.g. *an expert on astrology.*

    authority  buff *informal*  connoisseur  master specialist  virtuoso  whiz *informal*  wizard

## expire

(verb) When something expires, it reaches the end of the period of time for which it is valid.

e.g. *My bus pass expires next week.*

    end  finish  lapse  run out  stop  terminate

## explain

(verb) If you explain something, you give details about it or reasons for it so that it can be understood.

e.g. *He took them into a restaurant and explained the situation.*

    clarify  demonstrate  elucidate  expound illuminate  interpret  spell out

## expose

(verb) To expose a person or situation means to reveal the truth about them, especially when it involves dishonest or shocking behaviour.

e.g. *Johnson was exposed as a cheat.*

    bring to light  debunk  denounce  disclose divulge  reveal  show up  uncover  unmask

## extra

(adjective) more than is usual, necessary, or expected.

e.g. *an extra portion of salad.*

    added  additional  further  more  supplementary

## extraordinary

(adjective) unusual or surprising.

e.g. *an extraordinary feat of courage.*

exceptional phenomenal rare remarkable
singular surprising uncommon unusual

# *F f*

## fabric

**1.** (noun) Fabric is cloth.

e.g. *a crisp cotton fabric.*

    cloth   material

**2.** The fabric of a society or system is its structure, laws, and customs.

e.g. *The priests upheld the fabric of Roman society.*

    constitution   foundations   framework   organization
    structure

## fabulous

**1.** (adjective) wonderful or very impressive.

e.g. *They missed a fabulous opportunity.*

    amazing   astounding   breathtaking   immense
    incredible   phenomenal

**2.** not real, but happening or mentioned in stories or legends.

e.g. *fabulous animals and birds.*

    apocryphal   imaginary   legendary   mythical

## face

(noun) Your face is the front part of your head from your chin to your forehead.

e.g. *masks which protect the face.*

    countenance   features   physiognomy   visage

## facility

(noun) A facility is a service, opportunity, or piece of equipment which makes it possible to do something.

e.g. *excellent shopping facilities.*

  amenity   service

## fact

(noun) A fact is something that is true or has actually happened.

e.g. *I don't know if the rumour is based on facts or not.*

  act   deed   fait accompli *French*   happening
  incident   occurrence

## factor

(noun) A factor is something that helps to cause a result.

e.g. *House dust mites are a major factor in asthma.*

  cause   component   consideration   element
  influence   point

## fade

(verb) If something fades, the intensity of its colour, brightness, or sound is gradually reduced.

e.g *faded photographs.*

  bleach   decline   die out   dim   discolour   dissolve
  dwindle   ebb   melt away   vanish

## fail

(verb) If someone fails to achieve something, they are not successful.

e.g. *If I fail it is not the end of the world.*

  be disappointed   fall short   flop   founder   misfire
  miss

## failure

(noun) A failure is an unsuccessful person, thing, action, or event.

e.g. *The venture was a complete failure.*

collapse defeat disappointment fiasco flop incompetent loser loss washout wreck

## faint

**1.** (adjective) Something that is faint has little strength or intensity.

e.g. *There was a faint smell of gas.*

dim faded feeble hazy indistinct low slight soft subdued vague weak

**2.** (verb) If you faint, you lose consciousness for a short time.

e.g. *Due to tiredness I often faint.*

black out collapse keel over pass out swoon

## fair

(adjective) reasonable or equal according to generally accepted ideas about what is right and just.

e.g. *fair and prompt trials for political prisoners.*

disinterested dispassionate equal equitable honest impartial just objective unbiased

## faith

(noun) Faith is a feeling of confidence, trust or optimism about something.

e.g. *I have little faith in the human race.*

confidence conviction reliance trust

## faithful

(adjective) loyal to someone or something and remaining firm in support of them.

e.g. *a faithful friend.*

> constant dependable devoted loyal reliable
> staunch steadfast true trusty

## fake

**1.** (noun) A fake is an imitation of something made to trick people into thinking that it is genuine.

e.g. *a convincing fake of a 1930s radio.*

> copy forgery fraud hoax imitation phoney
> reproduction sham

**2.** (adjective) Fake means imitation and not genuine.

e.g. *fake fur.*

> bogus counterfeit false fraudulent imitation
> phoney reproduction sham

**3.** (verb) If you fake an emotion or feeling, you pretend that you are experiencing it.

e.g. *faking grief.*

> counterfeit fabricate feign pretend put on
> simulate

## false

**1.** (adjective) untrue, mistaken, or incorrect.

e.g. *The accusation is false and unjust.*

> erroneous inaccurate incorrect mistaken
> unfounded wrong

**2.** not real or genuine but intended to seem real.

e.g. *false teeth.*

artificial  bogus  counterfeit  fake  imitation  mock
reproduction  sham  synthetic

## fame

(noun) Fame is the state of being very well known.

e.g. *It is hard to find fame as a novelist.*

celebrity  eminence  glory  prominence  renown
reputation  stardom

## familiar

**1.** (adjective) well known or easy to recognize.

e.g. *familiar faces.*

common  customary  everyday  ordinary
recognizable  stock  well known

**2.** knowing or understanding something well.

e.g. *Most children are familiar with the story of
Cinderella.*

au fait  conversant  knowledgeable  well up on

## famous

(adjective) very well known.

e.g. *a famous actress.*

celebrated  eminent  honoured  illustrious
legendary  notable  noted  prominent  renowned

## fan

(noun) If you are a fan of someone or something, you
like them very much and are very enthusiastic about
them.

e.g. *a football fan.*

enthusiast  follower  supporter

## fanatic

(noun) A fanatic is a person who is very extreme in their support for a cause or in their enthusiasm for a particular sport or activity.

e.g. *a religious fanatic.*

> addict bigot buff devotee diehard enthusiast extremist visionary zealot

## fanatical

(adjective) If you are fanatical about something, you are very extreme in your enthusiasm or support for it.

e.g. *a fanatical patriot.*

> bigoted burning extreme fervent frenzied immoderate obsessive overenthusiastic passionate rabid wild zealous

## fancy

(adjective) Something that is fancy is special and elaborate.

e.g. *dressed up in some fancy clothes.*

> elaborate elegant extravagant fanciful flowery intricate ornate

## fantastic

(adjective) wonderful and very pleasing.

e.g. *a fantastic view of the sea.*

> brilliant fabulous marvellous sensational stupendous superb wonderful

## far

1. (adjective) Far means very distant.

e.g. *in the far south of England.*

> deep distant outlying remote

**2.** (adverb) Far also means very much or to a great extent or degree.

e.g. *far more important.*

   considerably decidedly greatly incomparably
   much

## far-fetched

(adjective) unlikely to be true.

e.g. *The theory is too far-fetched to be considered.*
   doubtful dubious implausible improbable
   preposterous unconvincing unrealistic

## fascinate

(verb) If something fascinates you, it interests and
delights you so much that your thoughts concentrate
on it and nothing else.

e.g. *a film that fascinates.*

   absorb beguile bewitch captivate charm
   delight enchant engross enthral entrance
   intrigue

## fashion

(noun) A fashion is a style of dress or way of
behaving that is popular at a particular time.

e.g. *the fashion for tight clothing.*

   craze fad latest mode rage style trend usage
   vogue

## fashionable

(adjective) Something that is fashionable is very
popular with a lot of people at the same time.

e.g. *the fashionable new drink.*

   à la mode current in in vogue happening latest

modern   popular   prevailing   trendy   up-to-date

## fast

(adjective) moving, doing something, or happening quickly or with great speed.

e.g. *fast communications.*

brisk   flying   hasty   hurried   quick   rapid   speedy
swift

## fasten

(verb) To fasten something means to close it, do it up, or attach it firmly to something else.

e.g. *They were fastening a rope to a tree.*

affix   attach   bind   bolt   fix   latch   lock   seal
secure   tie

## fat

(adjective) Someone who is fat has too much weight on their body.

e.g. *a fat girl.*

corpulent   gross   heavy   obese   overweight
plump   podgy   portly   roly-poly   rotund   stout
tubby

## fatal

**1.** (adjective) very important or significant and likely to have an undesirable effect.

e.g. *The mistake was fatal to my plans.*

calamitous   catastrophic   disastrous   ruinous

**2.** causing death.

e.g. *a fatal accident.*

deadly   lethal   malignant   mortal   terminal

## fate

(noun) Fate is a power that is believed to control events.

e.g. *Fate was kind to Tara.*

 chance destiny fortune predestination providence

## fault

(noun) A fault in something or in someone's character is a weakness or imperfection in it.

e.g. *She was blind to his faults.*

 blemish defect drawback failing flaw imperfection shortcoming weakness

## faulty

(adjective) If something is faulty, it has something wrong with it.

e.g. *We traced the trouble to a faulty transformer.*

 broken defective imperfect inaccurate malfunctioning out of order wrong

## favourite

**1.** (adjective) Your favourite person or thing is the one you like best.

e.g. *She's one of my favourite writers.*

 dearest favoured preferred

**2.** (noun) Someone's favourite is the person or thing they like best.

e.g. *Chocolate was his favourite.*

 choice dear idol pet preference

## favouritism

(noun) Favouritism is behaviour in which you are unfairly more helpful or more generous to one person than to other people.

e.g. *his favouritism towards his younger daughter.*

bias favour partiality preference prejudice

## fear

(noun) Fear is an unpleasant feeling of danger.

e.g. *the fear of crime.*

alarm dread fright nightmare panic phobia terror trepidation

## feather

(noun) A feather is one of the light fluffy structures covering a bird's body.

e.g. *ruffled ostrich feathers.*

plumage plume

## feature

**1.** (noun) A feature of something is an interesting or important part or characteristic of it.

e.g. *Career guidance discussions were a feature of our final year.*

aspect facet factor point

**2.** A feature is an article or programme dealing with a particular subject.

e.g. *a feature on drug abuse.*

article column item piece report story

**3.** (verb) To feature something means to include it or emphasise it as being important.

e.g. *The film features two of my favourite actors.*
    accentuate emphasise promote spotlight

## feeble

(adjective) lacking power, strength, or influence.

e.g. *The management was feeble and cowardly.*
    effete failing infirm powerless puny weak

## feel

(verb) If you feel that something is the case, you believe it to be so.

e.g. *She feels that she is in control of her life.*
    believe consider deem perceive sense think

## feeling

(noun) Your feelings about something are your general attitudes, impressions, or thoughts about it.

e.g. *Americans have quite a different feeling about the press.*
    idea impression instinct notion opinion perception view

## fellowship

(noun) Fellowship is a feeling of friendliness that a group of people have when they are doing things together.

e.g. *Classes gathered together in fellowship.*
    brotherhood camaraderie fraternity intimacy

## fertile

(adjective) able to produce something easily or in large amounts.

e.g. *in the realm of her fertile imagination.*

flowering fruitful plentiful productive prolific
rich teeming

## festival

(noun) A festival is a day or period of religious
celebration.

e.g. *a Buddhist festival.*

carnival celebration feast fiesta holiday

## festive

(adjective) full of happiness and celebration.

e.g. *at Christmas or other festive occasions.*

celebratory convivial gala happy

## feverish

(adjective) suffering from a high body temperature.

e.g. *a fevered brow.*

burning fevered flushed hot inflamed

## fib

(noun) A fib is a small, unimportant lie.

e.g. *a fib about her exact age.*

lie prevarication story white lie

## fidgety

(adjective) If you are fidgety, you keep changing your
position because you are nervous or bored.

e.g. *The children are starting to get fidgety.*

impatient jittery jumpy nervous restive restless
uneasy

## field

(noun) A field is an area of land where crops are
grown or animals are kept.

e.g. *We put the donkey in a field.*

grassland meadow pasture

## fiendish

**1.** (adjective) very clever and imaginative.

e.g. *a fiendish plan.*

ingenious masterful

**2.** very difficult and challenging.

e.g. *fiendish mazes.*

daunting devilish diabolical tricky unspeakable
wicked

## fierce

(adjective) very aggressive or angry.

e.g. *a fierce personal attack.*

dangerous feral ferocious menacing savage
threatening vicious violent

## fight

**1.** (verb) When people fight, they take part in a
battle, a war, a boxing match, or in some other
attempt to hurt or kill someone.

e.g. *Riot police fought with crowds.*

brawl come to blows grapple scrap skirmish
struggle tussle wrestle

**2.** (noun) A fight is a situation in which people hit or
try to hurt each other.

e.g. *The man was killed in a fight.*

battle brawl conflict fracas free-for-all scrap
scrimmage scuffle skirmish tussle

## fill

(verb) If you fill something, it becomes full.

e.g. *a large hall filled with rows of desks.*

cram crowd pack pervade stock stuff swell

## filth

(noun) Filth is disgusting dirt and muck.

e.g. *dust and filth on her skin.*

contamination dirt filthiness grime muck
nastiness squalor

## filthy

**1.** (adjective) Something that is filthy is disgustingly dirty.

e.g. *a really filthy oven.*

dirty foul grimy grubby mucky putrid squalid

**2.** morally unpleasant or disgusting, often about sexual matters.

e.g. *That's a filthy thing to say.*

coarse depraved dirty foul-mouthed impure
indecent lewd obscene pornographic smutty
suggestive

## final

**1.** (adjective) last in a series or happening at the end of something.

e.g. *the final year of school.*

closing concluding last terminating ultimate

**2.** Something that is final cannot be changed or questioned.

e.g. *The judges' decision is final.*

absolute  conclusive  definite  definitive
incontrovertible  irrevocable  settled

## finale

(noun) The finale is the last section of a piece of
music or show.

e.g. *the finale of Shostakovich's Fifth Symphony.*

climax  close  conclusion  culmination

## finally

**1.** (adverb) If something finally happens, it happens
after a long delay.

e.g. *She finally left her room.*

at last  at length  eventually  in the end  ultimately

**2.** You use the word finally to introduce a final
point, question, or topic that you are talking or
writing about.

e.g. *Finally, a word about the New Forest.*

in conclusion  in summary  lastly  to conclude

## financial

(adjective) relating to or involving money.

e.g. *financial problems.*

economic  fiscal  monetary  money  pecuniary

## find

(verb) If you find someone or something, you
discover them, either as a result of searching or by
coming across them unexpectedly.

e.g. *I need to find a job.*

come across  discover  encounter  espy  locate
meet  recognize  spot  unearth

## finish

**1.** (verb) When you finish something, you reach the end of it and complete it.

e.g. *I've finished my project.*

complete  conclude  discharge  end  execute  fulfil  wind up  wrap up

**2.** When something finishes, it ends or stops.

e.g. *The conversation finished.*

cease  close  conclude  stop  terminate

**3.** (noun) The finish of something is the end or last part of it.

e.g. *from the start of his career to the finish.*

cessation  close  completion  conclusion  ending

## fire

**1.** (noun) Fire is the flames produced when something burns.

e.g. *damage by fire.*

blaze  flames

**2.** A fire is a pile or mass of burning material.

e.g. *a house fire.*

conflagration  inferno

## firm

**1.** (adjective) Something that is firm does not move if it is pushed or shaken.

e.g. *Bake the cake for about an hour till the surface is risen and firm.*

compact  congealed  fixed  hard  inelastic  secure  solid  stable  tight  unshakable

**2.** Something that is firm is definite and unlikely to change.

e.g. *They want a firm decision by next Monday.*

> definite   fixed   inflexible   resolute   strict   unyielding

## first

(adjective) happening, coming, or done before everything or everyone else.

e.g. *That's the first thing to remember.*

> chief   earliest   foremost   fundamental   key
> leading   opening   original   pre-eminent   primary
> principal

## fit

**1.** (verb) If something fits a particular situation, person, or thing, it is suitable or appropriate.

e.g. *a sentence that fitted the crime.*

> accord with   correspond   go   match   meet   suit

**2.** (noun) If someone has a fit, their muscles suddenly start contracting violently and they may lose consciousness.

e.g. *He had an inexplicable fit.*

> convulsion   paroxysm   seizure   spasm

## fix

(verb) If you fix something broken, you mend it.

e.g. *He fixed the door.*

> mend   repair   secure

## flabby

(adjective) Someone who is flabby is rather fat and unfit, with loose flesh on their body.

e.g. *She was plump and rather flabby.*

flaccid  out of condition  sagging  slack  unfit

## flag

(noun) A flag is a rectangle or square of cloth of a particular colour and design which is used as the symbol of a nation, or as a signal.

e.g. *the British flag.*

banner  ensign  pennant  standard

## flashy

(adjective) expensive and fashionable in a rather vulgar way.

e.g. *a flashy car.*

flamboyant  garish  gaudy  jazzy *informal* loud  ostentatious  showy  tasteless

## flat

(adjective) Something that is flat is level and smooth.

e.g. *a bit of flat land.*

even  horizontal  level  unbroken

## flatter

(verb) If you flatter someone, you praise them in an exaggerated way, either to please them or to persuade them to do something.

e.g. *I knew she was just flattering me.*

butter up  cajole  fawn  sweet-talk

## flattery

(noun) Flattery is flattering words or behaviour.

e.g. *Blatant flattery will embarrass.*

blandishment  blarney  fawning  obsequiousness

sweet-talk

## flaw

**1.** (noun) A flaw is a fault or mark in a piece of fabric, china, or glass, or in a decorative pattern.

e.g. *a flaw in a stone.*

blemish  imperfection  mark  speck  spot

**2.** A flaw is also a weak point or undesirable quality in a theory, plan, or person's character.

e.g. *the flaw in my argument.*

blemish  defect  failing  fault  imperfection
weakness

## fleck

(noun) A fleck is a small coloured mark or particle.

e.g. *a fleck of paint.*

speck  speckle  spot

## flexible

**1.** (adjective) able to be bent easily without breaking.

e.g. *The tube is flexible but tough.*

elastic  pliable  pliant  springy

**2.** able to adapt to changing circumstances.

e.g. *a flexible arrangement.*

adaptable  adjustable  discretionary  open  variable

## flight

(noun) Flight is the action of flying or the ability to fly.

e.g. *the mysteries of flight.*

aviation  flying

## flinch

(verb) If you flinch, you make a sudden small movement in fear or pain.

e.g. *She flinched at the noise.*

blench  cringe  duck  quail  recoil  shrink  start
wince

## flirt

(verb) If you flirt with an idea, you consider it without seriously intending to do anything about it.

e.g. *I flirted with the idea of becoming a gambler.*

dally  play  toy

## flood

**1.** (noun) A flood is a large amount of water covering an area that is usually dry.

e.g. *a huge flood of rain.*

deluge  downpour  flash flood  inundation  spate
torrent

**2.** A flood of something is a large amount of it suddenly occurring.

e.g. *a flood of angry language.*

glut  profusion  rush  spate  stream  surge
swarm  tide

## floppy

(adjective) tending to hang downwards in a rather loose way.

e.g. *a floppy, outsize jacket.*

droopy  flaccid  limp  sagging  slack

## fluent

(adjective) able to express yourself clearly and without hesitation.

e.g. *fluent in several languages.*

    articulate  eloquent  flowing  voluble

## fly

(verb) When a bird, insect, or aircraft flies, it moves through the air.

e.g. *A small hawk flies near.*

    flit  flutter  glide  sail  soar

## foam

(noun) Foam is a mass of tiny bubbles.

e.g. *the white foam at the water's edge.*

    bubbles  froth  lather  spray  spume  suds

## foible

(noun) A foible is a minor eccentricity in a person's character.

e.g. *all sorts of human foibles.*

    eccentricity  idiosyncrasy  oddity  peculiarity  quirk

## foil

(verb) If you foil someone's attempt at something, you prevent them from succeeding.

e.g. *Their attempt to recapture Calais was foiled by a traitor.*

    balk  check  circumvent  defeat  frustrate  nullify  thwart

## fold

(verb) If you fold something, you bend it so that one part lies over another.

e.g. _He folded his napkin._

crease  double over  layer  overlap  pleat  tuck

## follow

(verb) Something that follows a particular thing happens after it.

e.g. _Night follows day._

ensue  succeed

## follower

(noun) The followers of a person or belief are the people who support them.

e.g. _a follower of Christ._

adherent  admirer  believer  devotee  disciple  fan  supporter

## folly

(noun) Folly is a foolish act or foolish behaviour.

e.g. _the extremes of human folly._

absurdity  foolishness  idiocy  imprudence  indiscretion  irrationality  lunacy  madness  nonsense  recklessness  stupidity

## fond

(adjective) If you are fond of someone or something, you like them.

e.g. _We are still very fond of each other._

adoring  affectionate  attached  caring  devoted  doting  indulgent  loving  tender

## food

(noun) Food is any substance consumed by an animal or plant to provide energy.

e.g. *daily food supplies.*

fare foodstuff nourishment provisions rations sustenance victuals

## fool

(noun) Someone who is a fool behaves in a silly way.

e.g. *She was not fool enough to think it would be easy.*

ass clot *informal* dunce dunderhead halfwit idiot ignoramus nincompoop simpleton twerp *informal* twit *informal*

## foolish

(adjective) very silly or unwise.

e.g. *foolish risks.*

absurd asinine harebrained idiotic ill-advised imprudent inane indiscreet injudicious ridiculous senseless short-sighted silly unreasonable unwise

## force

(verb) To force someone to do something means to make them do it.

e.g. *Don't force me to cook.*

bind coerce compel constrain dragoon drive impel make oblige pressurize

## forced

(adjective) Something that is forced is done with an effort and is not natural or spontaneous.

e.g. *a forced smile.*

artificial contrived false insincere laboured stiff
strained unnatural wooden

## foreign

(adjective) unfamiliar or uncharacteristic.

e.g. *Such daft enthusiasm was foreign to him.*

alien outlandish strange unfamiliar unknown

## forgive

(verb) If you forgive someone for doing something
bad, you stop feeling angry and resentful towards
them.

e.g. *He forgave her for past injuries.*

absolve excuse exonerate pardon

## formidable

(adjective) very difficult to deal with or overcome, and
therefore rather frightening or impressive.

e.g. *formidable enemies.*

challenging colossal daunting difficult
intimidating onerous overwhelming

## fort

(noun) A fort is a strong building built for defence.

e.g. *a fort overlooking the harbour.*

citadel fortress garrison stronghold

## forte

(noun) If something is your forte, you are particularly
good at doing it.

e.g. *Languages have never been your forte.*

métier speciality strength strong point

# fragile

(adjective) easily broken or damaged.

e.g. *a fragile ornament.*

breakable  brittle  delicate  flimsy  frail  weak

# fragrance

(noun) A fragrance is a sweet or pleasant smell.

e.g. *the fragrance of flowers.*

aroma  bouquet  perfume  scent  smell

# frank

(adjective) If you are frank, you say things in an open and honest way.

e.g. *a frank confession.*

blunt  candid  direct  downright  forthright  open
outright  outspoken  plain  sincere  straightforward

# free

**1.** (adjective) Someone who is free is no longer a prisoner.

e.g. *Three innocent men are free after years in prison.*

at large  at liberty  liberated  on the loose

**2.** If something is free, you can have it without paying for it.

e.g. *free drinks.*

complimentary  gratis  on the house

**3.** (verb) If you free something that is fastened or trapped, you release it.

e.g. *a campaign to free captive animals.*

extricate  loose  release  set free  turn loose
unleash  untie

**4.** When a prisoner is freed, he or she is released.

e.g. *Armed men freed her from prison.*

   discharge emancipate liberate release

## freedom

**1.** (noun) If you have the freedom to do something, you have the scope or are allowed to do it.

e.g. *freedom of speech.*

   carte blanche *French* discretion facility flexibility latitude leeway licence opportunity power scope

**2.** When prisoners gain their freedom, they escape or are released.

e.g. *her third day of freedom from prison.*

   emancipation liberty release

## frenzy

(noun) If someone is in a frenzy, their behaviour is wild and uncontrolled.

e.g. *a drunken frenzy.*

   agitation fever fit fury outburst paroxysm passion

## friend

(noun) Your friends are people you know well and like to spend time with.

e.g. *She and Hannah had been friends for years.*

   chum companion comrade confidant crony pal

## friendly

(adjective) If you are friendly to someone, you behave in a kind and pleasant way to them.

e.g. *The staff are experienced, friendly and helpful.*

affable  amiable  amicable  close  companionable
convivial  cordial  genial  intimate  sociable
sympathetic  welcoming  well-disposed

## friendship

(noun) Friendship is the state of being friends with
someone.

e.g. *I shared a warm friendship with Felicity.*

amity  camaraderie  closeness  friendliness
intimacy  rapport

## frighten

(verb) If something frightens you, it makes you afraid.

e.g. *The situation was beginning to frighten me.*

alarm  dismay  intimidate  petrify  scare  shock
startle  terrify  unnerve

## frivolous

(adjective) Someone who is frivolous behaves in a silly
or light-hearted way, especially when they should be
serious or sensible.

e.g. *his outwardly frivolous attitude.*

childish  empty-headed  flighty  flippant  juvenile
puerile  silly  superficial

## frolic

(verb) When animals or children frolic, they run
around and play in a lively way.

e.g. *Puppies frolic happily on the lawn.*

caper  cavort  frisk  gambol  play  prance  romp

## frozen

(adjective) If you are frozen, you are extremely cold.

e.g. *Savage was tired and frozen.*

chilled  frigid  ice-cold  icy  numb

## frugal

**1.** (adjective) Someone who is frugal spends very little money.

e.g. *Mary is severely frugal with herself.*

abstemious  careful  economical  parsimonious
prudent  saving  sparing  thrifty

**2.** A frugal meal is small and cheap.

e.g. *I had our frugal breakfast ready.*

insubstantial  meagre  niggardly

## frustrate

(verb) To frustrate something such as a plan means to prevent it.

e.g. *She hopes to frustrate the engagement of her son.*

balk  block  defeat  foil  forestall  stymie  thwart

## full

(adjective) containing or having as much as it is possible to hold.

e.g. *His room is full of posters.*

brimful  chock-a-block  chock-full  crammed
crowded  filled  gorged  jammed  loaded  packed
replete  sated  stocked

## fun

(noun) Fun is enjoyable lighthearted activity or amusement.

e.g. *That would have spoiled the fun.*

amusement diversion enjoyment entertainment gaiety jollity merrymaking pleasure recreation sport

## fund

(verb) Someone who funds something provides money for it.

e.g. *research funded by pharmaceutical companies.*

endow finance float promote sponsor subsidize support

## funny

1. (adjective) strange or puzzling.

e.g. *It's funny that you met the same people.*

curious mysterious odd peculiar perplexing puzzling queer remarkable rum strange suspicious unusual weird

2. causing amusement or laughter.

e.g. *a funny old film.*

amusing comic comical diverting droll entertaining farcical hilarious humorous jocular witty

## furniture

(noun) Furniture is movable objects such as tables, chairs and wardrobes.

e.g. *17th century oak furniture.*

effects fittings furnishings

## further

(verb) If you further something, you help it to progress.

e.g. *This success will certainly further your career.*
    advance  assist  champion  expedite  foster
    promote

## fuss

(noun) Fuss is unnecessarily anxious or excited
behaviour.

e.g. *They played with no fuss in the playroom.*
    ado  agitation  bother  bustle  commotion
    confusion  excitement  flurry  fluster  palaver  to-
    do  trouble

## fussy

(adjective) likely to fuss a lot.

e.g. *He was unusually fussy about keeping things perfect.*
    choosy  exacting  faddy  fastidious  finicky
    particular  pernickety  *informal*

## futile

(adjective) having no chance of success.

e.g. *a futile attempt to calm the storm.*
    abortive  fruitless  pointless  to no avail
    unavailing  unproductive  unprofitable
    unsuccessful  useless  vain

# G g

**gadget**

(noun) A gadget is a small machine or tool.

e.g. *a new gadget that makes driving safer.*

appliance contraption *informal* device tool

**gamble**

**1.** (verb) When people gamble, they bet money or play games like roulette in order to try and win money.

e.g. *Many workers gamble on horses and greyhounds.*

bet wager

**2.** If you gamble something, you risk losing it in the hope of gaining an advantage.

e.g. *The company gambled everything on the new factory.*

chance hazard risk stake

**game**

(noun) A game is an enjoyable activity with a set of rules which is played by individuals or teams against each other.

e.g. *I spent the day reading and playing games.*

diversion pastime play recreation sport

**gap**

(noun) A gap is a space between two things or a hole in something solid.

e.g. *They squeezed through a gap in the fence.*

breach break chink cleft crack divide hole
opening space

## garbled

(adjective) Garbled messages are jumbled and the
details may be wrong.

e.g. *her garbled version of events.*

confused distorted

## gather

**1.** (verb) When people gather, they come together in
a group.

e.g. *Hundreds of people gathered at the scene.*

assemble collect congregate convene flock
group

**2.** If you gather a number of things, you collect them
or bring them together in one place.

e.g. *He gathered up the rubbish and put it in a bag.*

amass assemble collect group marshal muster
round up

## gaudy

(adjective) very colourful in a vulgar way.

e.g. *gaudy T-shirts.*

bright flamboyant garish loud

## gauzy

(adjective) light, thin, and almost transparent.

e.g. *She was wearing a robe of some gauzy, shimmering
material.*

diaphanous filmy sheer wispy

## general

**1.** (adjective) relating to the whole of something or to most things in a group, rather than to separate parts.

e.g. *your general health.*

broad  overall

**2.** true, suitable, or relevant in most situations.

e.g. *the general opinion.*

common  extensive  overall  popular  prevailing prevalent  universal  widespread

## generous

**1.** (adjective) A generous person is very willing to give money, time, or gifts.

e.g. *Mrs Zuckerman is very generous with advice and information.*

free  lavish  liberal  munificent  open-handed

**2.** Something that is generous is very large.

e.g. *a generous helping of pudding.*

abundant  bountiful  lavish  liberal

## get

**1.** (verb) 'Get' often means the same as 'become'.

e.g. *She began to get suspicious.*

become  grow  turn

**2.** If you get something, you fetch it, receive it, or are given it.

e.g. *Get me a glass of water.*

acquire  bring  come by  fetch  obtain  procure secure

## get at

**1.** (verb) If someone is getting at you, they are criticizing you in an unkind way.

e.g. *He's been getting at me all day.*

attack  criticize  find fault with  pick on

**2.** If you ask someone what they are getting at, you are asking them to explain what they mean.

e.g. *I can't imagine what you're getting at.*

hint  imply  mean  suggest

## ghost

(noun) A ghost is the spirit of a dead person, believed to haunt people or places.

e.g. *It is said that his ghost still roams the grounds of the castle.*

phantom  soul  spectre  spirit  spook *informal*
wraith

## give

(verb) If you give someone something, you hand it to them or provide it for them.

e.g. *I gave him some money.*

bestow  confer  furnish  grant  impart  present
provide  supply

## give in

(verb) If you give in, you admit that you are defeated.

e.g. *We argued for a while, but eventually I gave in.*

admit defeat  submit  surrender  yield

## glib

(adjective) speaking or spoken quickly and confidently but without sincerity.

e.g. *a glib reply.*

    quick  ready  slick  smooth  smooth-tongued

## gloss

(noun) Gloss is a bright shine on a surface.

e.g. *This polish gives a wonderful gloss to wood.*

    lustre  sheen  shine

## glossy

(adjective) smooth and shiny.

e.g. *glossy hair.*

    lustrous  shining  shiny  sleek  smooth

## glower

(verb) If you glower, you stare angrily.

e.g. *They glowered at each other across the table.*

    frown  glare  scowl

## go

**1.** (verb) If you go, you move or travel from one place to get to another.

e.g. *I wasn't going to go until he arrived.*

    depart  journey  leave  set off  travel  withdraw

**2.** If something goes well, it is successful. If it goes badly, it is unsuccessful.

e.g. *All will go well as long as you trust your intuition.*

    fare  happen  proceed  result  turn out  work out

**3.** If a machine or clock goes, it works and is not

broken.

e.g. *This clock goes for months on one little battery.*
function operate perform run work

**4.** (noun) A go is an attempt at doing something.

e.g. *Isn't it fun having a go at a foreign language?.*
attempt crack *informal* shot *informal* stab
*informal* try turn whack *informal*

## go on

**1.** (verb) If you go on doing something, you continue to do it.

e.g. *I couldn't go on living with him.*
carry on continue keep on persist proceed

**2.** Something that is going on is happening.

e.g. *We looked out to see what was going on.*
happen occur

## go through

(verb) If you go through an unpleasant event, you experience it.

e.g. *I wouldn't go through that again for all the tea in China.*

bear endure experience suffer tolerate undergo

## gobble

(verb) If you gobble food, you eat it very quickly.

e.g. *He gobbled all the beef stew.*

bolt devour gorge guzzle scoff wolf

## good

**1.** (adjective) pleasant, acceptable, or satisfactory.

e.g. *a good night's sleep.*

> acceptable excellent fine first-class first-rate great pleasant satisfactory splendid super *informal*

**2.** skilful or successful.

e.g. *a good goalscorer.*

> able accomplished adept capable competent efficient expert proficient skilled talented

**3.** well-behaved.

e.g. *He was a good boy when he was young.*

> mannerly obedient polite well-behaved well-mannered

**4.** (noun) Good is moral and spiritual justice and rightness.

e.g. *the eternal struggle between good and evil.*

> goodness morality right righteousness virtue

**5.** Good also refers to anything that is desirable, useful, or beneficial as opposed to harmful.

e.g. *It is a decision she has made for the good of the company.*

> advantage benefit gain profit welfare well-being

## goodbye

(interjection) You say 'Goodbye' when you are leaving someone or ending a telephone conversation.

e.g. *I said goodbye and walked away.*

> adieu cheerio *informal* farewell

## grab

**1.** (verb) If you grab something, you take it or pick it up roughly.

e.g. _She grabbed the suitcase._

clutch  grasp  grip  seize  snatch

**2.** If you grab an opportunity, you take advantage of it eagerly.

e.g. _He grabbed the chance to launch a blistering attack._

grasp  seize  snatch

## grace

(noun) Grace is an elegant way of moving.

e.g. _She walked with grace._

charm  elegance  gracefulness  poise

## grain

**1.** (noun) A grain of sand or salt is a tiny particle of it.

e.g. _A single grain of sand can wreck a camcorder's tape deck._

granule  particle  speck

**2.** A grain of a quality is a tiny amount of it.

e.g. _There was a grain of truth in his story._

iota  particle  speck

## grand

(adjective) magnificent in appearance and size.

e.g. _a grand palace._

august  fine  great  imposing  impressive  lofty
magnificent  majestic  noble  opulent  princely
regal  splendid  stately  striking

## grateful

(adjective) If you are grateful for something, you are glad you have it and want to thank the person who gave it to you.

e.g. *We are grateful for their support.*

appreciative   indebted   obliged   thankful

## gratitude

(noun) Gratitude is the feeling of being grateful.

e.g. *I wish to express my gratitude to Kathy.*

appreciation   gratefulness   indebtedness
thankfulness   thanks

## greedy

(adjective) wanting more of something, such as food, than you really need.

e.g. *I'm very greedy and can't resist second helpings.*

acquisitive   avaricious   gluttonous   grasping
insatiable   piggish   rapacious   selfish   voracious

## greet

(verb) If you greet someone, you say something friendly like 'hello' to them when you meet them.

e.g. *Charlie came bounding out to greet her.*

hail   salute

## grief

(noun) Grief is extreme sadness.

e.g. *her grief over her mother's death.*

heartache   heartbreak   misery   sadness   sorrow
woe

## grieve

(verb) If you grieve, you are extremely sad, especially because someone has died.

e.g. _Families grieved for the loss of their loved ones._

bemoan    bewail    lament    mourn    sorrow

## grind

(verb) If you grind something such as corn or pepper, you crush it into a fine powder.

e.g. _He's got one of those machines that grinds coffee beans._

crush    mill    pound    powder    pulverize

## groove

(noun) A groove is a deep line cut into a surface.

e.g. _a groove sliced into the wood._

channel    furrow    hollow    rut    score

## group

(noun) A group of things or people is a number of them that are linked together in some way.

e.g. _a small group of friends._

assembly    band    bevy    bunch    category    class
collection    crowd    gang    gathering    party

## grow

(verb) To grow means to increase in size, amount, or degree.

e.g. _The company has grown from a one-man business to a multinational corporation in only ten years._

develop    enlarge    expand    extend    increase
multiply    rise    spread    swell    wax    widen

## growth

(noun) When there is a growth in something, it gets bigger.

e.g. *the growth in political opposition.*

development   enlargement   expansion   extension
growing   increase   increment   rise

## gruelling

(adjective) difficult and tiring.

e.g. *a gruelling race.*

arduous   demanding   difficult   exhausting   fierce
grinding   hard   harsh   laborious   punishing
severe   stiff   strenuous   taxing   tiring   trying

## grumpy

(adjective) bad-tempered and fed-up.

e.g. *a grumpy old man.*

bad-tempered   gruff   ill-tempered   irascible
irritable   snappy   surly   testy   touchy

## guarantee

**1.** (verb) If something or someone guarantees something, they make it certain that it will happen.

e.g. *Freedom does not guarantee happiness.*

assure   ensure   promise   secure   warrant

**2.** (noun) If something is a guarantee of something else, it makes it certain that it will happen.

e.g. *a guarantee of safety.*

assurance   pledge   promise   security   warranty

## guard

**1.** (verb) If you guard a person or object, you stay near to them either to protect them or to make sure they do not escape.

e.g. *Sentries guarded the gates.*

cover defend escort mind patrol protect safeguard shield

**2.** (noun) A guard is a person or group of people who guard a person, object, or place.

e.g. *Two guards were stationed at the main entrance.*

escort lookout patrol protector sentinel sentry warden warder watchman

## guess

**1.** (verb) If you guess something, you form or express an opinion that it is the case, without having much information.

e.g. *He guessed the answer.*

conjecture estimate speculate suppose surmise

**2.** (noun) A guess is an attempt to give the correct answer to something without having much information.

e.g. *Have a guess what the time is.*

conjecture speculation supposition theory

## gullible

(adjective) easily tricked.

e.g. *Hunt had already fooled four gullible women.*

credulous foolish green innocent naive trusting unsuspecting

## gush

**I.** (verb) When liquid gushes from something, it flows out of it in large quantities.

e.g. *Rain gushed down the hillsides.*

    burst cascade flood flow jet pour run rush spout spurt stream

**2.** When people gush, they express admiration or pleasure in an exaggerated way.

e.g. *Agents gushed about the discovery.*

    effuse enthuse

## guts

(plural noun) Your guts are your internal organs, especially your intestines.

e.g. *I felt a pain in my guts.*

    bowels entrails innards intestines

# H h

## hackneyed

(adjective) A hackneyed phrase is meaningless because it has been used too often.

e.g. *hackneyed dialogue.*

    clichéd   overworked   stock

## hamper

(verb) If you hamper someone, you make it difficult for them to move or progress.

e.g. *He has been hampered by injuries.*

    encumber   fetter   handicap   hinder   hold up
    impede   limit   restrict   retard

## handicap

(noun) A handicap is a physical or mental disability.

e.g. *John was born with the handicap of having no proper arms.*

    disability   impairment   impediment

## handsome

(adjective) very attractive in appearance.

e.g. *a handsome young actor.*

    attractive   comely   good-looking

## hang

(verb) If you hang something somewhere, you attach it to a high point. If it is hanging there, it is attached by its top to something.

e.g. *His jacket hung from a hook behind the door.*

dangle drape suspend

# happen

(verb) When something happens, it occurs or takes place.

e.g. *The accident happened at midnight.*

befall come about occur transpire

# happy

(adjective) feeling, showing, or producing contentment or pleasure.

e.g. *a happy smile.*

blissful blithe cheerful content contented glad jolly joyful merry pleased

# hard

**1.** (adjective) Something that is hard is firm, solid, or stiff.

e.g. *a hard piece of cheese.*

firm rigid set solid stiff tough

**2.** requiring a lot of effort.

e.g. *hard work.*

arduous exacting exhausting laborious rigorous strenuous tough uphill

**3.** difficult.

e.g. *a hard problem.*

baffling complex complicated difficult intricate involved perplexing puzzling thorny

# harm

(verb) To harm someone or something means to injure or damage them.

e.g. *He did not intend to harm the child.*

damage hurt ill-treat injure maltreat wound

## harsh

(adjective) severe, difficult, and unpleasant.

e.g. *harsh criticism.*

cruel grim hard severe tough unpleasant

## hate

(verb) If you hate someone or something, you have a strong dislike for them.

e.g. *He hates driving in London.*

abhor abominate despise detest dislike loathe

## hateful

(adjective) extremely unpleasant.

e.g. *Robert had just come from a hateful school.*

abhorrent abominable despicable detestable horrible loathsome obnoxious odious

## haughty

(adjective) showing excessive pride.

e.g. *He behaved in a haughty manner.*

arrogant disdainful high and mighty lofty proud snobbish snooty *informal* supercilious

## health

(noun) Health is the normally good condition of someone's body and the extent to which it is free from illness.

e.g. *Vitamins are essential for health.*

fitness healthiness soundness wellbeing

## healthy

(adjective) Someone who is healthy is fit and strong and does not have any diseases.

e.g. *Healthy people rarely seek out a doctor.*

fit   hale   hardy   robust   sound   strong   well

## heap

(noun) A heap of things is a pile of them.

e.g. *a heap of scrap metal.*

lot   mass   mound   mountain   pile   stack

## hear

(verb) When you hear sounds, you are aware of them because they reach your ears.

e.g. *He heard the noise of a radio from another room.*

catch   listen to   overhear   perceive

## heed

(verb) If you heed someone's advice, you pay attention to it.

e.g. *Harry refused to heed the warning.*

mark   mind   note

## help

**1.** (verb) To help someone means to make something easier, better, or quicker for them.

e.g. *I helped him with his homework.*

aid   assist   oblige   support

**2.** (noun) If you need or give help, you need or give assistance.

e.g. *He wants some help with a bit of building work.*

aid   assistance   succour   support

**3.** A help is someone or something that helps you.

e.g. *He really is a good help.*

　　aid　assistance　benefit　support

## helpful

(adjective) If someone is helpful, they help you by doing something for you.

e.g. *Martin found the nurses extremely helpful.*

　　accommodating　cooperative　kind　obliging
　　supportive　useful

## hesitant

(adjective) If you are hesitant, you do not do something immediately because you are uncertain, worried, or embarrassed.

e.g. *I was a little hesitant about approaching too closely.*

　　doubtful　indecisive　irresolute　uncertain　unsure
　　vacillating　wavering

## hesitate

(verb) To hesitate means to pause or show uncertainty.

e.g. *She hesitated before replying.*

　　dither　falter　pause　vacillate　waver

## hide

(verb) To hide something means to put it where it cannot be seen, or to prevent it from being discovered.

e.g. *He was unable to hide his disappointment.*

　　bury　cloak　conceal　cover　mask　obscure
　　screen　secrete　stash　veil

## high

**1.** (adjective) tall or a long way above the ground.

e.g. *a high wall.*

elevated  lofty  soaring  steep  tall  towering

**2.** (adverb) at or to a height.

e.g. *The flag flew high on the main tower.*

aloft

## hike

**1.** (noun) A hike is a long country walk.

e.g. *a fifteen-mile hike.*

march  ramble  tramp  trek  walk

**2.** (verb) To hike means to walk long distances in the country.

e.g. *I hiked to the summit.*

march  ramble  tramp  trek  walk

## hilarious

(adjective) very funny.

e.g. *There are some really hilarious moments in this film.*

amusing  comical  funny  humorous  hysterical side-splitting  uproarious

## hint

**1.** (noun) A hint is a suggestion or clue about something.

e.g. *There was no hint of any foul play.*

clue  implication  indication  insinuation intimation  suggestion

**2.** A hint is also a helpful piece of advice.

e.g. *some useful hints to help them improve their ratings.*

advice  pointer  tip

**3.** (verb) If you hint at something, you suggest it indirectly.

e.g. *He liked to hint at deep secrets.*

allude  imply  insinuate  intimate  suggest

## hire

(verb) If you hire something, you pay money to be able to use it for a period of time.

e.g. *Occasionally, I will hire a video.*

charter  engage  lease  rent

## hit

(verb) To hit someone or something means to strike or touch them forcefully, usually causing hurt or damage.

e.g. *The car hit a tree.*

bang  bash *informal*  knock  smack  strike  thump  wallop *informal*  whack

## hoard

**1.** (verb) To hoard things means to save them even though they may no longer be useful.

e.g. *Helen had hoarded discarded woollens.*

collect  gather  save  stash  stockpile  store  treasure

**2.** (noun) A hoard is a store of things that has been saved or hidden.

e.g. *a hoard of treasure.*

cache  reserve  stash  stockpile  store  supply

## hoarse

(adjective) A hoarse voice sounds rough and unclear.

e.g. *a hoarse whisper.*

    croaky  gravelly  gruff  harsh  husky  rasping
    rough

## hold

**1.** (verb) To hold something means to carry, support, or keep it in place, usually with your hand or arms.

e.g. *I held the baby in my arms.*

    clasp  cling  clutch  cradle  grasp  grip

**2.** If you hold something such as a meeting, a party, or an election, you arrange it and cause it to happen.

e.g. *Mr Mason held a party to celebrate.*

    arrange  conduct  convene  have  run

## hold off

(verb) To hold something off means to prevent or delay it.

e.g. *We held off from testing the boat last year.*

    defer  delay  postpone  prevent  put off

## hold out

(verb) If you hold out, you stand firm and manage to resist opposition in difficult circumstances.

e.g. *The rebels could hold out for ten years.*

    carry on  continue  endure  hang on  last  stand
    fast

## hold up

(verb) If something holds you up, it delays you.

e.g. *The traffic was held up by a procession.*

delay   detain   hinder   slow down

## hole

(noun) A hole is an opening or hollow in something.

e.g. *a hole in the wall.*

aperture   cavity   gap   hollow   opening

## holy

**1.** (adjective) relating to God or to a particular religion.

e.g. *the holy city.*

divine   hallowed   religious   sacred

**2.** Someone who is holy is religious and leads a pure and good life.

e.g. *a very holy lady.*

devout   godly   pious   pure   religious   righteous
saintly   virtuous

## home

(noun) Your home is the building, place, or country in which you live or feel you belong.

e.g. *his home in Oxford.*

abode   dwelling   house   pad *slang*   residence

## homely

(adjective) simple, ordinary and comfortable.

e.g. *The room was small and homely.*

comfortable   cosy   snug

## honest

(adjective) truthful and trustworthy.

e.g. *honest friends and neighbours.*

above board  genuine  honourable  straight
trustworthy  truthful  upright  veracious

## honesty

(noun) Honesty is the quality of being truthful and
trustworthy.

e.g. *His honesty earned him a high reputation.*

honour  integrity  trustworthiness  truthfulness

## honorary

(adjective) An honorary title or job is given as a mark
of respect or honour, and does not involve the usual
qualifications, work, or payment.

e.g. *She was awarded an honorary degree.*

complimentary  nominal  titular

## hooligan

(noun) A hooligan is a noisy, destructive, and violent
young person.

e.g. *German courts are cracking down on hooligans.*

delinquent  lout  ruffian  vandal

## horrible

(adjective) causing shock, fear, or disgust.

e.g. *The Inspector had seen many horrible crimes.*

appalling  awful  dreadful  frightful  ghastly  grim
gruesome  hideous  horrendous  horrid  horrific
repulsive  revolting  shocking  terrible

## hug

**1.** (verb) If you hug someone, you put your arms
round them and hold them close to you.

e.g. *He wanted to pick up his child and hug her.*

clasp  cuddle  embrace  enfold

**2.** (noun) If you give someone a hug, you hold them close to you.

e.g. *She greeted me with a hug and kiss.*

cuddle  embrace

## huge

(adjective) extremely large in amount, size, or degree.

e.g. *a huge success.*

colossal  enormous  gargantuan  giant  gigantic
great  immense  large  mammoth  massive
tremendous  vast

## humble

**1.** (adjective) A humble person is modest and thinks that he or she has very little value.

e.g. *Andy was a humble and gentle man.*

lowly  modest  unassuming

**2.** Something that is humble is small or not very important.

e.g. *Just a splash of wine will transform a humble casserole.*

insignificant  modest  ordinary  simple
unimportant

## humid

(adjective) If it is humid, the air feels damp, heavy, and warm.

e.g. *Visitors can expect hot and humid conditions.*

clammy  damp  moist  muggy  steamy  sticky
sultry

## humiliate

(verb) To humiliate someone means to make them feel ashamed or appear stupid to other people.

e.g. *He set out to injure and humiliate victims.*

disgrace embarrass humble mortify shame

## humour

(noun) Humour is the quality of being funny.

e.g. *They discussed it with tact and humour.*

amusement comedy fun wit

## hungry

(adjective) needing or wanting to eat.

e.g. *My friends went to bed hungry.*

empty famished peckish *informal* ravenous starved starving

## hurry

**1.** (verb) To hurry means to move or do something as quickly as possible.

e.g. *She hurried through the empty streets.*

dash fly hasten rush scurry

**2.** (noun) Hurry is the speed with which you do something quickly.

e.g. *He was in a hurry to leave.*

haste quickness rush speed urgency

## hygiene

(noun) Hygiene is the practice of keeping yourself and your surroundings clean, especially in order to prevent the spread of disease.

e.g. *high standards of hygiene.*

cleanliness   sanitation

## hypnotize

(verb) To hypnotize someone means to put them into a state in which they seem to be asleep but can respond to questions and suggestions.

e.g. *Patients are hypnotized and encouraged to remember their past lives.*

entrance   mesmerize

## hysterical

(adjective) Someone who is hysterical is in a state of uncontrolled excitement, anger, or panic.

e.g. *Sharon was almost hysterical with anxiety.*

beside yourself   frantic   frenzied   mad
overwrought   uncontrollable

# *I i*

## idea

**1.** (noun) An idea is a plan, suggestion, or thought that you have after thinking about a problem.

e.g. *an idea for starting a business.*

feeling hunch impression inkling notion thought

**2.** An idea is also an opinion or belief.

e.g. *We've all got very different ideas about music.*

belief concept image interpretation notion opinion perception thought understanding view viewpoint

## idiot

(noun) If you call someone an idiot, you mean that they are stupid or foolish.

e.g. *He was an idiot to believe that he would win.*

ass fool halfwit imbecile moron *informal* nincompoop nitwit *informal* simpleton twit *informal*

## idiotic

(adjective) extremely foolish or silly.

e.g. *idiotic behaviour.*

asinine crass crazy dim fatuous foolish halfwitted inane senseless stupid

## ignorant

(adjective) If you are ignorant of something, you do not know about it.

e.g. *He seems totally ignorant of the rules of cricket.*

green *informal* inexperienced innocent oblivious unaware unconscious

## ill

(adjective) unhealthy or sick.

e.g. *He became ill with stomach ulcers.*

ailing indisposed off-colour poorly queasy queer sick under the weather *informal* unhealthy unwell

## illegal

(adjective) forbidden by the law.

e.g. *illegal betting.*

criminal illicit lawless unauthorized unconstitutional unlawful

## illness

(noun) An illness is a particular disease.

e.g. *childhood illnesses such as measles, mumps, and whooping cough.*

ailment complaint disease disorder indisposition malady sickness

## imagine

**1.** (verb) If you imagine something, you form an idea of it in your mind, or you think you have seen or heard it but you have not really.

e.g. *I just imagined I was in France or Germany.*

conceive conjure up envisage picture visualize

**2.** If you imagine that something is the case, you believe it is the case.

e.g. *I imagine he has a lot of sleep to catch up on.*

fancy think

## imitate

(verb) To imitate someone or something means to copy them.

e.g. *Benedict could imitate Israeli accents.*

ape copy echo emulate follow impersonate mimic mirror simulate

## imminent

(adjective) If something is imminent, it is going to happen very soon.

e.g. *Police said more arrests were imminent.*

forthcoming impending in the offing looming prospective

## impartial

(adjective) Someone who is impartial has a fair and unbiased view of something.

e.g. *Scientists can be expected to be impartial.*

detached disinterested equitable fair just neutral objective open-minded

## imperfect

(adjective) Something that is imperfect has faults or problems.

e.g. *an imperfect system.*

damaged defective faulty flawed impaired incomplete limited

## impersonal

(adjective) An impersonal feeling or action does not relate to any particular person.

e.g. *impersonal criticism of the firm.*

clinical   cold   detached   dispassionate   formal
inhuman   neutral   remote

## important

(adjective) Something that is important is very valuable, necessary, or significant.

e.g. *important new medical developments.*

eminent   foremost   grave   great   high   influential
leading   momentous   portentous   prominent
salient   serious   significant   substantial   urgent
weighty

## impose

(verb) If you impose something on people, you force it on them.

e.g. *The allies had imposed a ban on all flights over Iraq.*

enforce   establish   foist   inflict   introduce   lay   levy

## impression

**1.** (noun) An impression of someone or something is the way they seem to you.

e.g. *They give the impression of not working.*

effect   feeling   idea   impact   sense

**2.** An impression of an object is a mark or shape that it has left in something soft.

e.g. *the mark left by the impression of the shoe.*

imprint   stamp

## impressionable

(adjective) easy to influence.

e.g. *impressionable teenagers*.

receptive responsive suggestible susceptible vulnerable

## improbable

(adjective) not probable or likely to happen.

e.g. *an improbable tale*.

doubtful fanciful far-fetched implausible unbelievable unlikely

## impromptu

(adjective) An impromptu action is one done without planning or organization.

e.g. *impromptu choruses of 'Happy Birthday'*.

ad-lib extempore improvised off the cuff spontaneous unpremeditated unprepared

## improve

(verb) If something improves or if you improve it, it gets better or becomes more valuable.

e.g. *The weather had improved on the second day*.

ameliorate better correct develop enhance pick up polish progress upgrade

## inactive

(adjective) not doing anything.

e.g. *An operation on his spine has kept him inactive*.

dormant idle immobile inert latent quiescent unemployed unoccupied unused

## inadequate

(adjective) If something is inadequate, there is not enough of it, or it is not good enough in quality for a particular purpose.

e.g. *inadequate washing facilities.*

deficient imperfect incapable incomplete insufficient meagre poor scant sketchy skimpy sparse

## inappropriate

(adjective) not suitable for a particular purpose or occasion.

e.g. *It was quite inappropriate to ask such questions.*

improper incongruous out of place tasteless unseemly unsuitable untimely wrong

## incite

**1.** (verb) If you incite someone to do something, you encourage them to do it by making them angry or excited.

e.g. *The authorities incited a mob that burned down his house.*

drive egg on encourage goad inflame spur urge

**2.** If you incite trouble or violent behaviour, you encourage it by making people angry or excited.

e.g. *meetings which incite racial hatred.*

excite foment instigate provoke rouse stir up

## include

(verb) If one thing includes another, it has the second thing as one of its parts.

e.g. *The price includes postage and package.*

comprehend comprise contain cover embrace
encompass incorporate involve take in

## incomparable

(adjective) Something that is incomparable is so good
that it cannot be compared with anything else.

e.g. *castles of incomparable beauty.*

inimitable matchless paramount peerless
superlative supreme unequalled unrivalled

## inconsiderate

(adjective) If you are inconsiderate, you do not
consider other people's feelings.

e.g. *a selfish, inconsiderate husband.*

careless insensitive tactless thoughtless
unthinking

## incredible

(adjective) totally amazing or impossible to believe.

e.g. *The fire spread at an incredible speed.*

amazing implausible impossible inconceivable
preposterous unbelievable unimaginable
unthinkable

## independent

(adjective) Something that is independent happens or
exists separately from other people or things.

e.g. *Results are assessed by an independent panel.*

autonomous self-sufficient separate unrelated

## indicate

(verb) If something indicates something, it shows that
it is true.

e.g. *a gesture which clearly indicates his relief.*

denote evince imply manifest reveal show
signify suggest

## indirect

**1.** (adjective) An indirect route, flight, etc. does not
go in a straight line between two places and so takes a
longer time.

e.g. *The goods went by a rather indirect route.*

circuitous devious meandering roundabout
tortuous

**2.** An indirect answer, reference, etc. is one that does
not directly mention the thing that is actually meant.

e.g. *Her indirect queries were met with more denial.*

circuitous oblique rambling roundabout

## inexperienced

(adjective) lacking experience of a situation or activity.

e.g. *inexperienced drivers.*

amateur callow fresh green *informal* immature
new raw unskilled

## infectious

(adjective) spreading from one person to another.

e.g. *an infectious disease.*

catching contagious contaminating

## inferior

**1.** (adjective) having a lower position or worth less
than something else.

e.g. *inferior quality cassette tapes.*

bad lesser lower poor shoddy

**2.** (noun) Your inferiors are people in a lower position than you.

e.g. *We have never treated women as inferiors.*
  junior  subordinate

## infinite

(adjective) without any limit or end.

e.g. *There could be an infinite number of universes.*
  absolute  boundless  endless  eternal  limitless

## influence

**1.** (noun) Influence is power that a person has over other people.

e.g. *These two guys had a great influence on my life.*
  authority  clout *informal*  control  effect  hold
  leverage  power  pull  weight

**2.** (verb) To influence someone or something means to have an effect on them.

e.g. *It's all too easy to be influenced by your parents.*
  affect  bias  direct  guide  persuade  predispose
  sway

## inform

**1.** (verb) If you inform someone of something, you tell them about it.

e.g. *He informed her of his decision.*
  acquaint  advise  apprise  enlighten  notify  tell

**2.** If you inform on a person, you tell the police about a crime they have committed.

e.g. *Christa discovered that her husband had been informing on her.*

sneak *informal* tell on

## information

(noun) If you have information on or about something, you know something about it.

e.g. *Regional secretaries can provide information on local activities.*

data facts gen *informal* intelligence knowledge news report word

## infrequent

(adjective) If something is infrequent it does not happen often.

e.g. *his infrequent letters.*

occasional rare sporadic uncommon unusual

## ingratiate

(verb) If you ingratiate yourself with people, you try to make yourself popular with them, for example by always agreeing with them.

e.g. *He learned the skill of ingratiating himself with the right people.*

crawl curry favour fawn flatter grovel insinuate yourself toady

## inhabitant

(noun) The inhabitants of a place are the people who live there.

e.g. *the inhabitants of Glasgow.*

citizen denizen local native resident

## insincere

(adjective) Someone who is insincere pretends to have feelings which they do not really have.

e.g. *He says I'm the most insincere person he's ever met.*

artificial  devious  dishonest  dissembling  false
hypocritical  lying  phoney  shallow  two-faced

## insipid

(adjective) An insipid person or activity is dull and
boring.

e.g. *this insipid Australian comedy.*

banal  bland  colourless  drab  dry  dull  flat
lifeless  prosaic  spiritless  tame  tedious  vapid
wishy-washy

## insult

**1.** (verb) If you insult someone, you offend them by
being rude to them.

e.g. *The final straw came when Andrew insulted a
woman teacher.*

abuse  offend  outrage  slight  snub

**2.** (noun) An insult is a rude remark which offends
you.

e.g. *a racist insult.*

abuse  affront  indignity  insolence  offence
outrage  rudeness  slight

## integrate

**1.** (verb) If a person integrates into a group, they
become part of it.

e.g. *schemes which assisted the refugees to integrate into
the local economies.*

assimilate  blend  incorporate

**2.** To integrate things means to combine them so

that they become closely linked or form part of a whole idea or system.

e.g. *his plan to integrate the coal and steel industries.*

    coalesce combine fuse merge unite

## intelligence

(noun) A person's intelligence is their ability to understand and learn things quickly and well.

e.g. *She had intelligence, ambition and drive.*

    brains cleverness intellect mind reason understanding

## interfere

(verb) If you interfere in a situation, you try to influence it, although it does not really concern you.

e.g. *He urged the French government not to interfere in German affairs.*

    butt in intervene intrude meddle poke your nose in tamper

## interrogate

(verb) If you interrogate someone, you question them thoroughly to get information from them.

e.g. *The police arrested and interrogated him.*

    cross-examine examine grill pump question quiz

## interval

(noun) An interval is a short break during a play or concert.

e.g. *The cost of the ticket includes a glass of champagne during the interval.*

    break interlude intermission

**intervene**

(verb) If you intervene in a situation, you step in to prevent conflict between people.

e.g. *Police had intervened to try to stop protesters.*

arbitrate   intercede   mediate

**intonation**

(noun) Your intonation is the way that your voice rises and falls as you speak.

e.g. *his father's Austrian intonation.*

cadence   inflection   modulation

**introduction**

(noun) The introduction to a book is a piece of writing at the beginning of it, which usually discusses the book in some detail.

e.g. *a memorable passage in the introduction to his 'Collected Poems'.*

foreword   opening   preamble   preface   prologue

**intrude**

(verb) To intrude on someone or something means to disturb them.

e.g. *I don't want to intrude on your parents.*

barge in *informal*   encroach   gatecrash   interrupt
trespass

**invent**

1. (verb) If you invent a machine, device, or process, you are the first person to think of it or to use it.

e.g. *The hot-dog was invented in Coney Island by Charles Feltman.*

coin   conceive   create   design   devise   discover

formulate  originate

2. If you invent a story or an excuse, you make it up.

e.g. *He had invented an imaginary son.*

imagine  improvise  make up

## investigate

(verb) To investigate something means to try to find out all the facts about it.

e.g. *Gas board engineers were investigating the incident.*

examine  explore  follow up  look into  make inquiries  probe  search  sift

## invincible

(adjective) unable to be defeated.

e.g. *an invincible army.*

indestructible  indomitable  insuperable unbeatable

## irregular

(adjective) Something that is irregular is not smooth or straight, or does not form a regular pattern.

e.g. *The paint was drying in irregular patches.*

asymmetrical  broken  eccentric  erratic  fitful fluctuating  fragmentary  haphazard  intermittent occasional  patchy  random  shifting  spasmodic sporadic  variable  wavering

## irresponsible

(adjective) An irresponsible person does things without considering the consequences.

e.g. *an irresponsible driver.*

careless  feckless  reckless  thoughtless  wild

## irritate

(verb) If something irritates you, it annoys you.

e.g. *He irritated her by eating all the cream.*

aggravate anger annoy bother chafe
exasperate fret gall grate infuriate jar nettle
pester provoke ruffle vex

## issue

**1.** (noun) An issue is an important subject that
people are talking about.

e.g. *the issues at stake.*

affair argument concern matter point problem
question subject topic

**2.** (verb) If someone issues something, they officially
supply it.

e.g. *I was issued with a prison uniform.*

distribute give out supply

## item

**1.** (noun) An item is one of a collection or list of
things.

e.g. *The first item he bought was an alarm clock.*

aspect component consideration detail entry
matter particular point thing

**2.** An item is a newspaper or magazine article.

e.g. *an item on how to take carnation cuttings.*

account article feature piece report

# *Jj*

**jagged**

(adjective) sharp and spiky.

e.g. *He tore his coat on a jagged piece of metal.*

    ragged  serrated  sharp  spiked

**jail**

(noun) A jail is a building where people convicted of a crime are locked up.

e.g. *He spent six months in jail for burglary.*

    clink *slang*  jug *slang*  nick *British slang*
    penitentiary *U.S.*  prison

**jam**

(noun) If someone is in a jam, they are in a difficult situation.

e.g. *I'm in the same financial jam as you are.*

    fix *informal*  pickle *informal*  plight  predicament
    quandary  trouble

**jealous**

**1.** (adjective) If you are jealous of someone, you feel bitterness and anger towards them because of something they possess or something they have achieved.

e.g. *They're just jealous of your success.*

    covetous  envious  grudging  resentful

**2.** If you are jealous of something you have, you feel you must try to keep it from other people.

e.g. *He was a very jealous husband.*
    possessive

# jewel

(noun) A jewel is a precious stone used to decorate valuable ornaments or jewellery.

e.g. *a rare and irreplaceable jewel.*
    gem  gemstone

# jinks

(noun) High jinks is boisterous and mischievous behaviour.

e.g. *Bill's annual parties are notorious for high jinks.*
    fun and games  merrymaking

# job

(noun) A job is the work that someone does to earn money.

e.g. *He thought he might lose his job.*
    employment  livelihood  occupation  office
    position  post  profession  situation  trade  work

# join

**1.** (verb) When two things join, or when one thing joins another, they come together.

e.g. *This road joins the motorway at junction 16.*
    adhere  connect  couple  link  unite

**2.** If you join a club or organization, you become a member of it or start taking part in it.

e.g. *He joined the company ten years ago.*
    enlist  enrol  enter  sign up

**3.** To join two things means to fasten them.

e.g. *Join the two outside edges together.*

> add  cement  connect  couple  fasten  link  unite

## joke

**1.** (noun) A joke is something that you say or do to make people laugh, such as a funny story.

e.g. *Kennedy chipped in with a good joke.*

> gag *informal*  hoax  jest  prank  quip  wisecrack *informal*  witticism

**2.** (verb) If you are joking, you are teasing someone.

e.g. *Don't take her seriously, she was only joking.*

> chaff  jest  kid *informal*  tease  wind up *British slang*

## journey

(noun) A journey is the act of travelling from one place to another.

e.g. *a long day's journey there and back.*

> excursion  expedition  trip  voyage

## judge

**1.** (noun) A judge is someone who decides the winner in a contest or competition.

e.g. *The judges awarded him first place.*

> adjudicator  arbiter  referee  umpire

**2.** (verb) To judge a contest or competition means to decide on the winner.

e.g. *She judges at dog shows all over the country.*

> adjudge  adjudicate  referee  umpire

## jump

**1.** (verb) To jump means to spring off the ground or some other surface using your leg muscles.

e.g. *She tried to jump out of the window.*

    bound  leap  spring

**2.** To jump something means to spring off the ground and move over or across it.

e.g. *He jumped the fence and ran for his life.*

    clear  hurdle  vault

**3.** (noun) A jump is a spring into the air, sometimes over an object.

e.g. *a jump of 2.37 metres.*

    bound  leap  spring

## jut

(verb) If something juts out, it sticks out beyond or above a surface or edge.

e.g. *jagged rocks jutting out of the sea.*

    project  protrude  stick out

# *K k*

### keen

(adjective) Someone who is keen shows great eagerness and enthusiasm.

e.g. *a keen gardener.*

ardent  avid  eager  earnest  enthusiastic  zealous

### keep

**1.** (verb) To keep someone or something in a particular condition means to make them stay in that condition.

e.g. *We'll walk to keep warm.*

conserve  hold  maintain  preserve  retain  store uphold

**2.** If you keep something, you have it and look after it.

e.g. *a gun that he kept for his private use.*

carry  look after  possess  safeguard

### keepsake

(noun) A keepsake is something that someone gives you to remind you of a particular person or event.

e.g. *a rare picture of his father for a keepsake.*

memento  relic  reminder  souvenir  symbol  token

### kidnap

(verb) To kidnap someone means to take them away by force and demand a ransom in exchange for returning them.

e.g. *He'd been kidnapped for money.*

abduct capture hijack seize snatch

## kill

(verb) To kill a person, animal, or plant means to make them die.

e.g. *I couldn't kill a cat.*

annihilate assassinate butcher destroy dispatch execute exterminate extirpate massacre murder obliterate slaughter slay

## kin

(plural noun) Your kin are your relatives.

e.g. *The reasons for moving were to be nearer kin or friends.*

family kinsfolk relations relatives

## kind

**1.** (noun) A particular kind of thing is something of the same type or sort as other things.

e.g. *I don't like that kind of film.*

brand class sort species stamp type variety

**2.** (adjective) Someone who is kind is considerate and generous towards other people.

e.g. *There was a kind and understanding side to him.*

benevolent benign kindhearted magnanimous

## king

(noun) The king of a country is a man who is the head of state in the country, and who inherited his position from his parents.

e.g. *George became King in 1936.*

    monarch  ruler  sovereign

**knowledge**

(noun) Knowledge is all the information and facts that you know.

e.g. *professors of great knowledge.*

    enlightenment  instruction  intelligence  know-how
    learning  scholarship  science  tuition  wisdom

# *L l*

## labour

1. (noun) Labour is hard work.

e.g. *Technology has taken a lot of the hard labour out of housework.*

    drudgery effort exertion industry slog *informal* toil travail

2. (verb; an old-fashioned use) To labour means to work hard.

e.g. *We laboured for three quarters of an hour.*

    slave slog *informal* toil travail work

## lack

(noun) If there is a lack of something, it is not present when or where it is needed.

e.g. *They complained of the lack of safety provisions.*

    absence dearth deficiency paucity scarcity shortage want

## lag

(verb) To lag behind means to make slower progress than other people or processes.

e.g. *Britain still lags far behind other countries in engineering.*

    dawdle fall behind linger loiter straggle trail

## lame

(adjective) A lame excuse is weak and unconvincing.

e.g. *He mumbled some lame excuse about having gone to*

_sleep._

> feeble flimsy inadequate pathetic poor thin
> weak

## lament

(verb) To lament something means to express sorrow
or regret about it.

e.g. _He laments the demise of cricket playing in schools._

> bemoan bewail complain deplore grieve
> mourn regret sorrow wail weep

## language

(noun) Your language is the style in which you
express yourself.

e.g. _His language is often obscure._

> idiom lingo parlance speech style vocabulary
> wording

## lanky

(adjective) Someone who is lanky is tall and thin and
moves rather awkwardly.

e.g. _He leaned his lanky body over the desk._

> angular bony gangling gaunt spare tall thin

## last

**1.** (verb) If something lasts, it continues to exist or
happen.

e.g. _Her speech lasted for fifty minutes._

> continue endure go on hold out remain survive

**2.** (adjective) Something or someone who is last is
the latest or most recent in a series.

e.g. _The last customers left at midnight._

closing concluding final hindmost latest

## late

(adjective) If something or someone is late, they are after the expected or usual time.

e.g. *a late lunch at the hotel.*

behind belated delayed overdue slow tardy

## latent

(adjective) A latent quality is hidden at the moment, but may emerge in the future.

e.g. *a latent talent for drawing.*

dormant potential unrealized

## layabout

(noun; an informal word) A layabout is someone who is lazy and does not work.

e.g. *He is a morose, work-shy layabout.*

good-for-nothing idler laggard loafer vagrant

## layer

(noun) A layer is a single thickness of something.

e.g. *layers of clothing.*

coat ply row seam sheet stratum thickness
tier

## layout

(noun) The layout of something is the pattern in which it is arranged.

e.g. *He tried to recall the layout of the farmhouse.*

arrangement design draft format outline plan

## laze

(verb) If you laze, you relax and do no work.

e.g. *We spent a few days lazing around by the pool.*

idle  loaf  loll  lounge  relax  take it easy *informal*

## lazy

(adjective) idle and unwilling to work.

e.g. *He is too lazy to get up in the morning.*

idle  indolent  lethargic  shiftless  slack  slothful

## lead

**1.** (verb) If you lead someone somewhere, you go in front of them in order to show them the way.

e.g. *He led her to a vacant table.*

conduct  escort  guide  pilot  precede  steer
usher

**2.** Someone who leads a group of people is in charge of them.

e.g. *The Labour Party was led by Wilson.*

command  direct  govern  head  manage  preside
over  supervise

## learn

(verb) If you learn of something, you find out about it.

e.g. *She learnt of his death from his sister.*

detect  discern  discover  find  find out  gather
grasp  hear  pick up  understand

## learned

**1.** (adjective) A learned person has a lot of knowledge gained from years of study.

e.g. *a learned professor.*

    cultured  erudite  expert  scholarly

**2.** Learned books and journals are written about serious academic subjects.

e.g. *a stream of articles in learned journals.*

    academic  highbrow

## least

(noun) The least is the smallest possible amount of something.

e.g. *No one paid the least attention to him.*

    fewest  lowest  minimal  minimum  slightest
    tiniest

## leave

(verb) When you leave a place, you go away from it.

e.g. *He decided to leave Paris.*

    decamp  depart  desert  disappear  exit  go
    move  quit  relinquish  retire  withdraw

## legacy

(noun) A legacy is property or money that someone receives in the will of a person who has died.

e.g. *a legacy left to me by my uncle.*

    bequest  estate  heirloom  inheritance

## leisurely

(adjective) A leisurely action is done in an unhurried and calm way.

e.g. *a leisurely stroll.*

    comfortable  easy  gentle  lazy  relaxed  restful
    slow  unhurried

### lengthen

(verb) To lengthen something means to make it longer.

e.g. _I lengthened my stride._

elongate  expand  extend  prolong  protract
stretch

### lessen

(verb) If something lessens, it is reduced in amount, size, or quality.

e.g. _The wind's noise lessened._

abate  decline  decrease  deplete  diminish
dwindle  lighten  reduce  relax  shrink  slacken
wane  weaken

### let

(verb) If you let someone do something, you allow them to do it.

e.g. _Don't let other people take advantage of you._

allow  authorize  give permission  permit  sanction

### lethargic

(adjective) If you feel lethargic, you have no energy or enthusiasm.

e.g. _She became pale and lethargic._

apathetic  drowsy  dull  heavy  inactive  languid
listless  slothful  slow  sluggish  somnolent  torpid

### level

**1.** (adjective) A surface that is level is smooth and flat.

e.g. _She looked across absolutely level fields._

even  flat  horizontal  smooth

**2.** (noun) A level is a point on a scale which measures the amount, importance, or difficulty of something.

e.g. *the highest level of government.*

degree  grade  rank  stage  step

## lie

**1.** (verb) To lie means to say something that is not true.

e.g. *She lied about her age.*

equivocate  fabricate  fib  prevaricate

**2.** (noun) A lie is something you say which is not true.

e.g. *She told lies as often as she told the truth.*

fabrication  falsehood  fib  prevarication  untruth

## lift

**1.** (verb) To lift something means to move it to a higher position.

e.g. *She lifted the mug and took a long swallow.*

elevate  hoist  mount  pick up  raise

**2.** To lift a ban on something means to remove it.

e.g. *to lift all controls on textile imports.*

annul  cancel  end  relax  remove  rescind  revoke  stop

## light

**1.** (noun) Light is brightness from the sun, moon, fire, or lamps, that enables you to see things.

e.g. *the light of the moon.*

brilliance  glow  illumination  lighting  radiance

**2.** (verb) To light a fire means to make it start burning.

e.g. *They were lighting oil-lamps, torches and candles.*

    fire  ignite  kindle  set fire to

**3.** (adjective) A light object does not weigh very much.

e.g. *She was as light as a feather.*

    airy  delicate  flimsy  insubstantial  lightweight
    portable  slight  underweight

**4.** A light task is fairly easy.

e.g. *I've been doing a little light training.*

    easy  effortless  manageable  moderate  simple
    undemanding

## light-hearted

(adjective) Someone who is light-hearted is cheerful and has no worries.

e.g. *George can be a light-hearted character.*

    blithe  carefree  cheerful  chirpy  happy-go-lucky
    sunny  untroubled

## like

**1.** (verb) If you like something or someone, you find them pleasant.

e.g. *He likes classical music.*

    be fond of  be keen on  be partial to  care for
    enjoy

**2.** (preposition) If one thing is like another, it is similar to it.

e.g. *I saw a dog like ours on the beach.*

akin alike allied analogous corresponding
identical relating resembling same similar

## limit

(noun) A limit is a boundary or an extreme beyond
which something cannot go.

e.g. *The speed limit was 30 mph.*

bound boundary ceiling check curb deadline
end extent maximum restraint restriction

## liquid

(adjective) Something that is liquid is in the form of a
liquid.

e.g. *liquid nitrogen.*

fluid melted molten running runny thawed
watery

## list

**1.** (noun) A list is a set of words or items written one
below the other.

e.g. *a shopping list.*

catalogue directory file inventory register roll
schedule tally

**2.** (verb) If you list a number of things, you make a
list of them.

e.g. *Manufacturers will have to list all ingredients on the
label.*

catalogue enter enumerate file index itemize
note record register

## literal

(adjective) A literal translation from a foreign

language is one that has been translated exactly word for word.

e.g. *The literal meaning of contre-jour is 'against day'.*

exact   faithful   strict   verbatim   word for word

## little

(adjective) small in size or amount.

e.g. *little bottles of shampoo and shower gel.*

diminutive   mini   miniature   minute   petite   pygmy
small   tiny   wee

## live

(verb) If you live in a place, that is where your home is.

e.g. *My sister lives in Ulster.*

abide   dwell   inhabit   lodge   reside   settle   stay

## lively

(adjective) full of life and enthusiasm.

e.g. *a lively debate.*

active   brisk   bustling   busy   colourful   crowded
eventful   exciting   frisky   perky   racy   spirited
stimulating   stirring   vivacious   vivid

## loan

**1.** (noun) A loan is a sum of money that you borrow.

e.g. *a loan from the bank.*

advance   credit

**2.** (verb) If you loan something to someone, you lend it to them.

e.g. *I loaned them some clothes.*

advance   lend

## local

**1.** (adjective) Local means in, near, or belonging to the area in which you live.

e.g. *the local newspaper.*
  community district neighbourhood regional

**2.** (noun) The locals are the people who live in a particular area.

e.g. *The locals view the proposal with alarm.*
  inhabitant native resident

## location

(noun) A location is a place, or the position of something.

e.g. *the perfect location for a hotel.*
  place point position site situation venue
  whereabouts

## lone

(adjective) A lone person or thing is the only one in a particular place.

e.g. *a lone climber.*
  isolated single sole solitary solo
  unaccompanied

## long

**1.** (adjective) continuing for a great amount of time.

e.g. *There had been no rain for a long time.*
  drawn-out extended lengthy prolonged
  protracted

**2.** (verb) If you long for something, you want it very much.

e.g. *She longs to join an amateur dramatics class.*

pine wish yearn

## long-winded

(adjective) long and boring.

e.g. *a long-winded letter.*

garrulous lengthy rambling repetitious tedious verbose wordy

## look

**1.** (verb) If you look at something, you turn your eyes towards it so that you can see it.

e.g. *Taggart looked at his watch.*

behold contemplate gaze glance inspect observe peek peep regard scrutinize view

**2.** (noun) If you have a look at something, you look at it.

e.g. *I had a quick look round the place.*

glance glimpse peek peep sight

**3.** The look on your face is the expression on it.

e.g. *a look of surprise.*

appearance aspect countenance demeanour expression

## loosen

(verb) To loosen something means to make it looser.

e.g. *He loosened his collar.*

free slacken undo unfasten untie

## loot

**1.** (verb) To loot shops and houses means to steal money and goods from them during a battle or riot.

e.g. *Angry workers looted shops.*

    pillage plunder raid ransack sack

**2.** (noun) Loot is stolen money or goods.

e.g. *bags that looked to be full of loot.*

    booty haul prize spoils swag

## lost

(adjective) If something is lost, you cannot find it.

e.g. *golfers looking for lost balls.*

    astray disappeared gone mislaid misplaced
    missing vanished

## lot

(noun) A lot of something, or lots of something, is a large amount of it.

e.g. *a vegetarian diet including a lot of pasta.*

    abundance heaps loads many masses oodles
    piles plenty quantities scores

## loud

**1.** (adjective) A loud noise has a high volume of sound.

e.g. *a loud explosion.*

    blaring deafening noisy piercing raucous
    resounding rowdy sonorous stentorian *formal*
    strong

**2.** If you describe clothing as loud, you mean that it is too bright and tasteless.

e.g. *a loud checked shirt.*

    flamboyant flashy garish gaudy lurid
    ostentatious showy tacky tasteless vulgar

## love

**I.** (verb) If you love someone, you have strong emotional feelings of affection for them.

e.g. *He loved his wife and his children.*

adore  cherish  dote on  idolize  prize  treasure worship

**2.** (noun) Love is a strong feeling of affection for someone or something.

e.g. *a genuine love of literature.*

adulation  affection  ardour  devotion  fondness friendship  infatuation  liking  passion  rapture regard  tenderness  warmth

## lovely

(adjective) Very beautiful, attractive, and pleasant.

e.g. *the lovely old manor house.*

attractive  beautiful  charming  delightful enchanting  exquisite  pleasant  pretty

## lower

(adjective) Lower describes people and things that are less important than other people and things.

e.g. *clubs in the lower divisions.*

junior  lesser  minor  secondary  smaller subordinate

## luck

(noun) Luck is anything that seems to happen by chance and not through your own efforts.

e.g. *I found my way there by luck.*

accident  chance  destiny  fate  fluke  fortune prosperity  success  windfall

## lucky

**1.** (adjective) Someone who is lucky has a lot of good luck.

e.g. *He had always been lucky at cards.*

charmed   favoured   fortunate

**2.** Something that is lucky happens by chance and has good effects or consequences.

e.g. *a lucky escape.*

auspicious   fortuitous   fortunate   opportune
propitious

## lustful

(adjective) feeling or expressing strong sexual desire.

e.g. *lustful thoughts.*

lascivious   lecherous   lewd   licentious   prurient
salacious

## luxurious

(adjective) very expensive and full of luxury.

e.g. *The rooms were furnished with luxurious carpets.*

costly   expensive   lavish   opulent   rich   splendid
sumptuous

## luxury

(noun) A luxury is something that you enjoy very much but do not have very often, usually because it is expensive.

e.g. *the luxury of breakfast in bed.*

extra   extravagance   indulgence   treat

## lying

(adjective) A lying person often tells lies.

e.g. *He is a lying scoundrel!*.

    deceitful  dishonest  false  mendacious  untruthful

# M m

## machine

(noun) A machine is a piece of equipment which uses electricity or power from an engine.

e.g. *a technician in white who sat next to a large noisy machine.*

> apparatus appliance contrivance device structure

## mad

**1.** (adjective) Someone who is mad has a mental illness which often causes them to behave in strange ways.

e.g. *They'd say she was mad, or, worse, she was making it up.*

> demented deranged insane unbalanced unhinged

**2.** If you describe someone as mad, you mean that they are very foolish.

e.g. *You must be mad to go out there alone.*

> crazy foolhardy foolish imprudent senseless

## magic

(noun) Magic is the art of performing tricks to entertain people.

e.g. *We're trying to find someone to do some magic at the children's party.*

> conjuring illusion sleight of hand sorcery

trickery witchcraft

## main

(adjective) most important.

e.g. *a main road.*

central chief critical crucial essential foremost
head leading major premier primary prime
principal

## majority

(noun) The majority of people or things in a group is
more than half of the group.

e.g. *The majority of the electorate were illiterate.*

best part bulk mass preponderance

## make

**1.** (verb) To make something means to produce or
construct it, or to cause it to happen.

e.g. *In your place I should not make any sweeping
changes.*

accomplish assemble build compose construct
create fabricate fashion form generate
manufacture originate produce

**2.** If someone makes you do something, they force
you to do it.

e.g. *She makes us wash up.*

coerce compel constrain dragoon drive force
impel induce oblige

**3.** (noun) The make of a product is the name of the
company that manufactured it.

e.g. *'What make is your car?' -- 'It's a Datsun.'.*

brand kind model type

## makeshift

(adjective) temporary and of poor quality.

e.g. *The refugees were put into makeshift shelters.*

provisional  stopgap  temporary

## making

(noun) The making of something is the act or process of creating or producing it.

e.g. *The making of the wine needs skill and full attention.*

assembly  building  construction  creation
manufacture  production

## malevolent

(adjective; a formal word) wanting or intending to cause harm.

e.g. *Her stare was malevolent, her mouth a thin line.*

baleful  hostile  malicious  malign  malignant
pernicious  spiteful  vengeful  vicious  vindictive

## malice

(noun) Malice is a desire to cause harm to people.

e.g. *He could be ruthless, but there was no malice in him.*

animosity  bitterness  enmity  hate  hatred  ill will
malevolence  rancour  spite  venom  vindictiveness

## man

1. (noun) A man is an adult male human being.

e.g. *The young man stopped at the side of the road.*

bloke *informal*  chap *informal*  fellow  gentleman
guy *informal*  male

2. (plural noun) Human beings in general are sometimes referred to as men.

e.g. *All men are equal.*

humanity  mankind  mortals  people

## manage

(verb) If you manage to do something, you succeed in doing it.

e.g. *However did you manage to find me?.*

accomplish  arrange  contrive  cope  effect engineer  get by  succeed  survive

## management

(noun) The management of a business is the controlling and organizing of it.

e.g. *involvement in the management of local government.*

administration  control  running  supervision

## manner

**1.** (noun) The manner in which you do something is the way in which you do it.

e.g. *to behave in a more socially responsible manner.*

fashion  method  mode  style  system  technique way

**2.** Your manner is the way in which you behave and talk.

e.g. *The judge was impressed by his manner.*

air  appearance  approach  attitude  bearing behaviour  conduct  demeanour  deportment  look presence  tone

## marine

(adjective) relating to or involving the sea.

e.g. *marine life.*

maritime  nautical  naval  oceanic  seafaring

## marital

(adjective) relating to or involving marriage.

e.g. *marital problems.*

conjugal  married  matrimonial  wedded

## market

(noun) A market is a place where goods or animals are bought and sold.

e.g. *Bargaining, except in the odd market or antique shop, is no longer appropriate.*

bazaar  fair  mart

## marriage

(noun) Marriage is the act of marrying someone.

e.g. *a mixture of regret and happiness at her daughter's marriage.*

alliance  matrimony  union  wedding  wedlock

## matter

**1.** (noun) A matter is something that you have to deal with.

e.g. *I have given the matter much thought.*

affair  business  concern  episode  incident  issue
question  situation  subject  topic

**2.** (verb) If something matters to you, it is important.

e.g. *The wallpaper really did not matter a lot to him.*

be important  count  signify

## mean

**1.** (verb) If you mean to do something, you intend to do it.

e.g. *Sorry, I meant to write before.*

intend plan propose want wish

**2.** (adjective) Someone who is mean is unwilling to spend much money.

e.g. *Don't be mean with the tip.*

miserly niggardly parsimonious stingy tight tight-fisted

## meaning

(noun) The meaning of what someone says, or of a book or a film, is the thoughts or ideas that it is intended to express.

e.g. *Mark was old enough now to understand their meaning.*

content drift explanation gist implication import interpretation message point sense significance substance

## mediocre

(adjective) of rather poor quality.

e.g. *a mediocre string of performances.*

average indifferent middling ordinary passable pedestrian so-so tolerable undistinguished uninspired

## meek

(adjective) A meek person is timid and does what other people say.

e.g. *holding out his sword in meek surrender.*

acquiescent compliant deferential docile gentle humble mild modest submissive yielding

## meet

(verb) If you meet someone, you happen to be in the same place as them.

e.g. *We met her at the hotel.*

bump into  come across  confront  contact
encounter  find

## meeting

(noun) A meeting is an event in which people discuss proposals and make decisions together.

e.g. *the association's annual meeting.*

assembly  conference  convention  gathering  get-together  session

## melodious

(adjective) pleasant to listen to.

e.g. *soft melodious music.*

dulcet  mellifluous  musical  silvery  sweet-sounding  tuneful

## melodramatic

(adjective) behaving in an exaggerated, emotional way.

e.g. *She wanted to laugh at the melodramatic way he was behaving.*

dramatic  extravagant  histrionic  theatrical

## melt

(verb) When something melts or when you melt it, it changes from a solid to a liquid because it has been heated.

e.g. *watching the mounds of snow melt in the courtyard.*

dissolve  liquefy  soften  thaw

## memory

(noun) A memory is something you remember about the past.

e.g. *childhood memories.*

recollection remembrance reminiscence

## mention

(verb) If you mention something, you talk about it briefly.

e.g. *She told me something then that Tim had never mentioned.*

allude bring up broach cite refer to

## merchandise

(noun; a formal word) Merchandise is goods that are sold.

e.g. *He had left me with more merchandise than I could sell.*

commodities goods produce products stock wares

## merchant

(noun) A merchant is a trader who imports and exports goods.

e.g. *a textile merchant.*

dealer retailer purveyor salesman supplier trader vendor

## merciful

(adjective) showing kindness and forgiveness.

e.g. *It's the most merciful way there is.*

compassionate forbearing forgiving gracious humane kind lenient sparing

## merciless

(adjective) showing no kindness or forgiveness.

e.g. *calling for the merciless elimination of enemy commando units.*

    heartless  implacable  inexorable  pitiless
    relentless  remorseless  ruthless  unfeeling

## mercy

(noun) If you show mercy, you show kindness and forgiveness and do not punish someone as severely as you could.

e.g. *There was no thought of mercy, only of revenge.*

    clemency  compassion  forbearance  forgiveness
    leniency  pity  quarter

## merriment

(noun) Merriment is happiness, laughter, and fun.

e.g. *As midnight drew near, merriment waxed fierce and furious.*

    amusement  conviviality  festivity  fun  gaiety
    glee  hilarity  jollity  laughter  mirth  revelry

## mess

**1.** (noun) If something is a mess, it is untidy.

e.g. *They make a terrible mess when they're here.*

    chaos  clutter  confusion  disarray  disorder  hash
    *informal* jumble  shambles  untidiness

**2.** If a situation is a mess, it is full of problems and trouble.

e.g. *Edwards was already sorry he had got himself into this mess.*

    difficulty  dilemma  fix *informal* jam *informal* mix-up  muddle  pickle *informal*  predicament

## messenger

(noun) A messenger is someone who takes a message to someone for someone else.

e.g. *A messenger delivered an envelope at the office.*

courier  emissary  envoy  go-between

## mild

(adjective) Mild weather is warmer than usual.

e.g. *We've had two mild winters.*

balmy  clement  temperate  warm

## miserable

**1.** (adjective) If you are miserable, you are very unhappy.

e.g. *Now everything's gone wrong and I feel helpless and miserable.*

dejected  depressed  despondent  disconsolate distressed  doleful  downcast  gloomy  lugubrious melancholy  mournful  sorrowful  unhappy woebegone  wretched

**2.** If a place or a situation is miserable, it makes you feel depressed.

e.g. *a squalid, miserable little bed-sit.*

depressing  dismal  gloomy  poor  shabby  sordid squalid  wretched

## mistake

(noun) A mistake is an action or opinion that is wrong or is not what you intended.

e.g. *Annoyed, he realized he had made a mistake.*

blunder error fault faux pas gaffe
misunderstanding oversight slip solecism

# mix

(verb) If you mix things, you combine them or shake
or stir them together.

e.g. *I don't like mixing business and pleasure.*

amalgamate blend combine merge mingle

# mixture

(noun) A mixture of things consists of several
different things put together.

e.g. *Alan looked at him with a mixture of incredulity and
fear.*

alloy amalgam assortment blend combination
compound concoction conglomeration medley
miscellany mix variety

# mock

**1.** (verb) If you mock someone, you say something
scornful or imitate their foolish behaviour.

e.g. *Sometimes they mocked her, calling out behind her
back.*

deride gibe jeer make fun of ridicule scoff
sneer taunt wind up *informal*

**2.** (adjective) not genuine.

e.g. *mock Tudor houses.*

artificial fake imitation sham spurious

# mockery

(noun) Mockery is the expression of scorn for
someone or ridicule of their foolish behaviour.

e.g. *He looked impressed, but was there a glint of mockery in his eyes?.*

> contempt  derision  jeering  ridicule  scorn

## model

(noun) Something that is described as, for example, a model of clarity or a model of perfection, is extremely clear or absolutely perfect.

e.g. *This garment, which was already a model of neatness, was straightened out.*

> archetype  epitome  example  ideal  paragon
> pattern  prototype  standard

## modern

**1.** (adjective) relating to the present time.

e.g. *the social problems of modern society.*

> contemporary  current  present-day

**2.** new and involving the latest ideas and equipment.

e.g. *modern technology.*

> latest  new  present  up-to-date

## moment

(noun) A moment is a very short period of time.

e.g. *She hesitated for a moment.*

> instant  jiffy  minute  second

## money

(noun) Money is the coins or banknotes that you use to buy something.

e.g. *Jim bought a house with the money.*

> capital  cash  currency  funds

## mood

**1.** (noun) Your mood is the way you are feeling at a particular time.

e.g. *I'm in a really good mood.*
    frame of mind   humour   temper

**2.** The mood of a group of people is the way they think or feel about something.

e.g. *A mood of pessimism grew amongst the delegates.*
    air   atmosphere   tenor   vein

## moody

**1.** (adjective) Someone who is moody is depressed or unhappy.

e.g. *retreating into moody silence.*
    gloomy   glum   morose   petulant   sulky   sullen

**2.** Someone who is moody often changes their mood for no apparent reason.

e.g. *This type of personality can be moody and difficult.*
    temperamental   touchy

## motivate

(verb) If you are motivated by something, it causes you to behave in a particular way.

e.g. *people motivated by a lust for power and money.*
    actuate   drive   impel   induce   inspire   move
    prompt   stimulate

## move

**1.** (verb) To move means to go to a different place or position..

e.g. *Can you move down the bus, please?.*

budge  go  proceed  stir  walk

**2.** To move something means to change its place or position.

e.g. *Workmen were moving a heavy wardrobe.*

carry  shift  transport

## muddle

**1.** (noun) A muddle is a state of disorder or untidiness.

e.g. *My papers are all in a muddle.*

chaos  clutter  confusion  disarray  disorder
hotchpotch  mess  mix-up  tangle

**2.** (verb) If you muddle things, you mix them up.

e.g. *The work became hopelessly muddled.*

confuse  jumble  mix up

## murder

(noun) Murder is the deliberate and unlawful killing of a person.

e.g. *investigating the murder of the MP.*

assassination  bloodshed  homicide  killing
slaughter

## murmur

**1.** (verb) If you murmur, you say something very softly.

e.g. *Across the room she sensed that her mother murmured something to John.*

mumble  mutter  whisper

**2.** (noun) A murmur is an utterance which can hardly be heard.

e.g. *The sergeants spoke in low murmurs.*
> babble buzz drone humming muttering purr
> rumble undertone whisper

## musical

(adjective) Musical sounds are pleasant and tuneful.

e.g. *His voice was soft and soothing, almost musical.*
> dulcet harmonious lilting lyrical melodious
> tuneful

## mysterious

1. (adjective) strange and not well understood.

e.g. *a mysterious phenomenon known as corn circles.*
> abstruse arcane baffling curious inexplicable
> obscure recondite secret strange uncanny
> weird

2. secretive about something.

e.g. *You've been very mysterious lately; what's going on?.*
> cryptic enigmatic furtive

# *N n*

### narrow-minded

(adjective) unwilling to consider new ideas or opinions.

e.g. *I'm not too narrow-minded in my outlook.*

   bigoted hidebound insular narrow parochial

### nasty

(adjective) very unpleasant.

e.g. *Ella spat out the name as if it had a nasty taste.*

   disagreeable disgusting foul horrible loathsome
   nauseating objectionable odious offensive
   repellent repugnant unpleasant vile

### natural

**1.** (adjective) not trying to pretend or hide anything.

e.g. *talking in a relaxed, natural manner.*

   artless candid frank genuine ingenuous open
   real simple spontaneous unaffected

**2.** A natural ability is one you were born with.

e.g. *her natural talent for singing.*

   inborn inherent innate instinctive intuitive
   native

### naval

(adjective) relating to or having a navy.

e.g. *naval bases.*

   marine maritime nautical

#### necessary

(adjective) Something that is necessary is needed or must be done.

e.g. *harsh but necessary measures.*

> compulsory essential imperative mandatory needful obligatory required requisite vital

#### need

(noun) Your needs are the things that you need to have.

e.g. *Shoes are needs, not luxuries.*

> demand essential necessity requirement requisite want

#### needless

(adjective) unnecessary.

e.g. *needless cruelty.*

> gratuitous groundless pointless redundant superfluous uncalled-for

#### nervous

(adjective) worried and frightened.

e.g. *I felt very nervous about travelling.*

> agitated anxious apprehensive edgy fearful fidgety jittery *informal* jumpy neurotic on edge tense uptight worried

#### new

**1.** (adjective) recently made or created.

e.g. *a new plan.*

> brand-new different fresh improved latest modern modernized newfangled novel up-to-date

**2.** not known, used, or encountered before.

e.g. *a part of England completely new to her.*

unfamiliar  unknown  virgin

## next

(adjective) coming immediately after something else.

e.g. *They lived in the next street.*

adjacent  adjoining  consequent  ensuing
following  later  neighbouring  subsequent
succeeding

## nice

(adjective) pleasant or attractive.

e.g. *He's such a nice young man.*

agreeable  attractive  charming  delightful  good
likable  pleasant

## nobility

(noun) The nobility of a society are all the people
who have titles and high social rank.

e.g. *The nobility retained its social influence.*

aristocracy  nobles  peerage  peers  upper classes

## noise

(noun) A noise is a sound, especially one that is loud
or unpleasant.

e.g. *The children make a dreadful noise.*

clamour  commotion  din  hubbub  pandemonium
racket  row  sound  tumult  uproar

## nominate

(verb) If you nominate someone for a job or position,
you formally suggest that they have it.

e.g. *candidates who had been nominated for the programme.*

> assign  designate  name  propose  recommend  suggest

## nonsense

(noun) Nonsense is foolish and meaningless words or behaviour.

e.g. *Don't talk nonsense.*

> absurdity  bilge *informal*  bombast  drivel  folly  rot  rubbish  stupidity  trash  twaddle

## normal

(adjective) usual and ordinary.

e.g. *I try to lead a normal life.*

> average  natural  ordinary  routine  typical  usual

## notice

**1.** (verb) If you notice something, you become aware of it.

e.g. *We all noticed an improvement.*

> detect  discern  distinguish  heed  mind  note  observe  perceive  see  spot

**2.** (noun) Notice is attention or awareness.

e.g. *I'm glad he brought it to my notice.*

> attention  observation

## notorious

(adjective) well-known for something bad.

e.g. *The area has become notorious for violence against tourists.*

> disreputable  infamous  scandalous

## nuisance

(noun) A nuisance is someone or something that is
annoying or inconvenient.

e.g. *Our dog was causing a nuisance by barking.*

bore  bother  drag *informal*  hassle  inconvenience
irritation  pest  problem  trouble  vexation

## number

(noun) A number is a word or a symbol used for
counting or calculating.

e.g. *the numbers one, two, and three.*

digit  figure  numeral

# O o

**oaf**

(noun) An oaf is a clumsy and stupid person.

e.g. *He was irascible and earthy, something of an oaf.*

boor   brute   lout

**oath**

(noun) An oath is a formal promise, especially a promise to tell the truth in a court of law.

e.g. *They were ready to swear on oath that Cantrell had known about it.*

avowal   pledge   vow

**obese**

(adjective) extremely fat.

e.g. *He has become obese and lazy.*

corpulent   fat   fleshy   gross   heavy   outsize
plump   podgy   portly   rotund   stout

**obey**

(verb) If you obey a person or an order, you do what you are told to do.

e.g. *All visitors must obey the rules.*

abide by   comply   conform   discharge   execute
follow   fulfil   heed   keep   mind   observe   perform
respond

**object**

(verb) If you object to something, you dislike it or disapprove of it.

e.g. *Politicians of all parties objected to the way the article questioned their patriotism and resolve.*

demur  expostulate  oppose  protest  take exception

## obscene

(adjective) indecent and offensive.

e.g. *obscene pictures.*

bawdy  blue  coarse  dirty  disgusting  filthy  foul immoral  improper  impure  indecent  lewd offensive  pornographic  salacious  suggestive

## obscure

(adjective) Something obscure is difficult to see or to understand.

e.g. *The news was shrouded in obscure language.*

abstruse  arcane  confusing  cryptic  deep mysterious  opaque  recondite  unclear

## obsession

(noun) If someone has an obsession about something, they cannot stop thinking about that thing.

e.g. *Antiques were his obsession.*

fetish  fixation  mania  phobia  preoccupation thing *informal*

## obsolete

(adjective) out of date and no longer used.

e.g. *The original concept of limited war had been rendered obsolete by changing political circumstances.*

antiquated  archaic  bygone  dated  defunct extinct  outmoded  passé

## obstacle

(noun) An obstacle is something which is in your way and makes it difficult to do something.

e.g. *The price was also something of an obstacle.*

bar barrier block check hindrance hitch hurdle obstruction stumbling block

## obstinate

(adjective) Someone who is obstinate is stubborn and unwilling to change their mind.

e.g. *She is a very strong-willed child and can be very obstinate.*

determined dogged immovable inflexible intractable intransigent pig-headed stubborn unyielding

## obvious

(adjective) easy to see or understand.

e.g. *"All right," he said with obvious reluctance.*

apparent blatant clear conspicuous distinct evident manifest overt palpable patent perceptible plain pronounced transparent unmistakable

## oddments

(plural noun) Oddments are things that are left over after other things have been used.

e.g. *She filled it with oddments that she fancied might be useful on the journey.*

odds and ends remnants

## offer

(verb) If you offer something to someone, you ask them if they would like it.

e.g. *He looked as if he too would gladly offer help.*

    proffer  suggest  tender  volunteer

## ogle

(verb) To ogle someone means to stare at them in a way that indicates a sexual interest.

e.g. *spitting tobacco juice and ogling the passing ladies.*

    eye up  leer

## ointment

(noun) An ointment is a smooth thick substance that you put on sore skin to heal it.

e.g. *applying antibiotic cream or ointment.*

    balm  cream  embrocation  liniment  lotion  salve

## okay

(adjective; an informal word) Okay means all right.

e.g. *Tell me if this sounds okay.*

    acceptable  adequate  not bad  passable
    satisfactory  so-so  tolerable

## old

(adjective) having lived or existed for a long time.

e.g. *old clothes.*

    aged  age-old  ancient  antiquated  antique
    dated  decrepit  elderly  grey  mature  senile
    venerable  worn-out

## old-fashioned

(adjective) Something which is old-fashioned is no longer fashionable.

e.g. *old-fashioned shoes.*

> ancient antiquated archaic bygone dated dead obsolete outmoded passé past

## omen

(noun) An omen is something that is thought to be a sign of what will happen in the future.

e.g. *John saw this success as a good omen for his trip to Luxembourg.*

> indication portent sign

## ominous

(adjective) suggesting that something unpleasant is going to happen.

e.g. *an ominous sign.*

> dark forbidding menacing sinister threatening unfavourable

## opening

1. (noun) An opening is a hole or gap.

e.g. *A small opening is left at the top.*

> aperture breach break cleft crack gap hole mouth orifice space

2. An opening is also an opportunity.

e.g. *an opening in show business.*

> chance occasion opportunity place vacancy

## opinion

(noun) An opinion is a belief or view.

e.g. *The general opinion was that war would not come.*

belief  estimation  feeling  idea  judgment  view

## opposite

(noun) If two things are completely different, they are opposites.

e.g. *Whatever you think their response will be you can expect to hear the opposite.*

antithesis  contradiction  contrary  contrast
converse  inverse  reverse

## oppress

(verb) To oppress people means to treat them cruelly or unfairly.

e.g. *resolved to raise issues that specifically oppress women.*

afflict  burden  crush  harass  harry  persecute
subjugate  tyrannize

## oral

(adjective) spoken rather than written.

e.g. *oral history.*

spoken  verbal  vocal

## ordeal

(noun) An ordeal is a difficult and extremely unpleasant experience.

e.g. *the ordeal of being arrested and charged with attempted murder.*

affliction  agony  hardship  nightmare  suffering
trial  tribulation

## order

1. (noun) An order is a command.

e.g. *Quickly she gave her orders.*

> command decree dictate direction directive
> injunction instruction

2. If things are done in a particular order, they are done in that sequence.

e.g. *in alphabetical order.*

> arrangement array grouping layout pattern
> plan sequence

## orderly

(adjective) Something that is orderly is well organized or arranged.

e.g. *the children standing in an orderly line behind their father.*

> businesslike controlled decorous disciplined
> methodical neat regular shipshape systematic
> tidy

## ordinary

(adjective) Ordinary means not special or different in any way.

e.g. *I'm wearing an ordinary shirt and slacks.*

> average common commonplace conventional
> customary everyday familiar household
> mundane normal pedestrian regular routine
> standard stock typical usual workaday

## organization

(noun) An organization is any group, society, club, or business.

e.g. *Lie low - don't join any student body or organization.*

> association body company concern consortium corporation group grouping league network syndicate

## origin

(noun) You can refer to the beginning or cause of something as its origin or origins.

e.g. *traces of its nineteenth century origins.*

> beginning birth dawning derivation emergence foundation genesis roots source

## outline

(noun) The outline of something is its shape.

e.g. *the vague outline of the distant mountains.*

> contour form profile shape silhouette

## overjoyed

(adjective) extremely pleased.

e.g. *Francis was overjoyed to see him.*

> delighted elated joyful jubilant rapturous thrilled

## overrule

(verb) To overrule a person or their decisions means to decide that their decisions are incorrect.

e.g. *The Home Secretary refused to overrule the decision.*

> annul cancel countermand invalidate override rescind reverse revoke veto

## own

(verb) If you own something, it belongs to you.

e.g. *Sam owned a chain of liquor stores.*
enjoy  have  hold  keep  possess  retain

# $P\,p$

### pacify

(verb) If you pacify someone who is angry, you calm them.

e.g. *The chairman was trying to pacify the audience.*

appease  conciliate  mollify  placate  soothe

### pain

(noun) Pain is an unpleasant feeling of physical hurt or deep unhappiness.

e.g. *a sharp, stabbing pain.*

ache  hurt  pang  smart  sting  suffering
tenderness  torment  twinge

### paltry

(adjective) If something is paltry, it is very small or insignificant.

e.g. *a paltry contribution.*

beggarly  contemptible  derisory  insignificant
miserable  sorry  trifling  wretched

### paper

(noun) A paper is an article on a particular subject presented at a conference or in a journal.

e.g. *supervisors adding their names to a paper without contributing to the work.*

article  dissertation  report  thesis  treatise

## paralyse

(verb) If something paralyses you, it causes loss of feeling and movement in your body.

e.g. *a poison dart designed to paralyse its victim.*

freeze immobilize incapacitate numb petrify transfix

## paraphrase

(verb) If you paraphrase what someone has said, you express it in a different way.

e.g. *He paraphrased my comments about the course.*

interpret rephrase restate reword

## pardonable

(adjective) If you describe someone's bad behaviour as pardonable, you mean that you understand why they did it and think that they should be forgiven.

e.g. *This was an exaggeration, but a pardonable one.*

excusable forgivable understandable venial

## parody

(noun) A parody is an amusing imitation of the style of an author or of a familiar situation.

e.g. *It was intended as a parody of a chat show.*

burlesque caricature imitation lampoon satire skit spoof takeoff travesty

## part

(noun) A part of something is one of the pieces, sections, or aspects that it consists of.

e.g. *a new six-part TV series.*

aspect bit component constituent element fragment member piece section

## participate

(verb) If you participate in an activity, you take part in it.

e.g. *The audience will be encouraged to participate.*
engage in  join in  partake  share  take part

## pass

**1.** (verb) To pass something means to move past it.

e.g. *I pass a bakery on the way to work every day.*
go by *or* past  move past  proceed

**2.** When a period of time passes, it happens and finishes.

e.g. *You're having a bad time just now, but it will pass.*
elapse  go by  lapse

## passing

(adjective) lasting only for a short time.

e.g. *a passing phase.*
brief  ephemeral  fleeting  momentary  short-lived
temporary  transient  transitory

## passion

(noun) Passion is a very strong feeling, especially of sexual attraction.

e.g. *There's no passion at all in their marriage.*
ardour  fervour  fire  force  intensity  lust  rapture
vehemence  warmth

## passionate

(adjective) expressing very strong feelings about something.

e.g. *his deep knowledge and passionate love of his subject.*

amorous ardent fervent fiery frenzied hot-blooded impassioned intense vehement warm wild

## passive

(adjective) remaining calm and showing no feeling when provoked.

e.g. *Women are brought up to think of themselves as passive and weak.*

compliant inactive inert quiescent submissive

## pastime

(noun) A pastime is a hobby or something you do just for pleasure.

e.g. *His favourite pastime is golf.*

activity hobby interest pursuit recreation

## pathetic

(adjective) weak, inadequate, or helpless.

e.g. *the most pathetic and heart-rending story of the war.*

affecting forlorn moving pitiable pitiful plaintive poignant sorry touching

## patience

(noun) Patience is the ability to stay calm in a difficult or irritating situation.

e.g. *No man's patience is infinite.*

forbearance restraint stoicism tolerance

## pay

(verb) When you pay money to someone, you give it to them because you are buying something or owe it to them.

e.g. *Lewis didn't offer to pay for any of it.*

recompense  reimburse  settle  square up

## peace

(noun) Peace is a state of undisturbed calm and quiet.

e.g. *I will never forget the peace of that summer morning.*

calm  concord  harmony  quiet  repose  serenity
tranquillity

## peaceful

(adjective) quiet, calm, and free from disturbance.

e.g. *a small luxurious hotel in peaceful surroundings.*

calm  harmonious  placid  quiet  restful  serene
tranquil

## peak

(noun) The peak of an activity or process is the point
at which it is strongest or most successful.

e.g. *He's at the peak of his career.*

acme  apex  climax  culmination  height  pinnacle
summit  zenith

## peeved

(adjective; an informal word) irritated and annoyed.

e.g. *She looked a little peeved at being left out.*

annoyed  exasperated  irked  irritated  piqued  put
out  riled  sore  vexed

## peevish

(adjective) irritable and complaining.

e.g. *He looked surprised at my peevish retort.*

cantankerous  complaining  fractious  fretful
petulant  plaintive  querulous

## pensive

(adjective) deep in thought.

e.g. *Patterson was in a particularly pensive mood.*

contemplative  dreamy  meditative  preoccupied
reflective  thoughtful

## pent-up

(adjective) Pent-up emotions have been held back for
a long time without release.

e.g. *giving vent to her pent-up feelings.*

bottled-up  repressed  smothered  stifled
suppressed

## people

**1.** (plural noun) People are men, women, and
children.

e.g. *They murdered hundreds of people.*

folk  human beings  humanity  mortals  persons

**2.** (noun) A people is all the men, women, and
children of a particular country or race.

e.g. *the peace and harmony on which the welfare of a
people depends.*

citizens  nation  populace  population  public  race

## perceive

(verb) If you perceive something that is not obvious,
you see it or realize it.

e.g. *I began to perceive the advantages of this
arrangement.*

discern  distinguish  make out  note  notice
observe  remark  spot

## perceptive

(adjective) Someone who is perceptive realizes or notices things that are not obvious.

e.g. *an intelligent and perceptive man.*

acute  astute  discerning  observant  penetrating
percipient  perspicacious

## perfect

**1.** (adjective) of the highest standard and without fault.

e.g. *His English was perfect.*

consummate  faultless  flawless  ideal
immaculate  impeccable

**2.** (verb) If you perfect something, you make it as good as it can possibly be.

e.g. *Engineers were working to perfect a rocket.*

hone  polish  refine

## permeate

(verb) To permeate something means to spread through it and affect every part of it.

e.g. *The feeling of failure permeates everything I do.*

impregnate  penetrate  percolate  pervade  seep
suffuse

## permissible

(adjective) allowed by the rules.

e.g. *restraints on what is permissible for publication.*

admissible  allowable  authorized  legitimate
permitted  proper  sanctioned

## permission

(noun) If you have permission to do something, you are allowed to do it.

e.g. *There is no possibility of getting planning permission.*

authorization  clearance  consent  dispensation
go-ahead  leave  licence  sanction

## permit

(verb) To permit something means to allow it or make it possible.

e.g. *His wife would not permit an autopsy.*

allow  authorize  entitle  grant  let  license
sanction

## persecute

(verb) To persecute someone means to treat them with continual cruelty and unfairness.

e.g. *We do not want to persecute minority groups.*

badger  bait  hound  oppress  pick on  pursue
torment  victimize

## persevere

(verb) If you persevere, you keep trying to do something and do not give up.

e.g. *He is determined to persevere with his medical studies.*

carry on  continue  go on  keep going  persist
stick at

## person

(noun) A person is a man, woman, or child.

e.g. *I'm not at all a violent person.*

character  human  human being  individual  soul

## personal

(adjective) Personal means belonging or relating to a particular person rather than to people in general.

e.g. *my personal feeling.*

    exclusive individual own particular private

## persuade

(verb) If someone persuades you to do something or persuades you that something is true, they make you do it or believe it by giving you very good reasons.

e.g. *Do ads persuade you to buy a certain product?.*

    coax convince entice get induce prevail upon win over

## perverted

(adjective) Someone who is perverted has disgusting or unacceptable behaviour or ideas, especially sexual behaviour or ideas.

e.g. *the product of a sick and perverted mind.*

    abnormal deviant kinky sick twisted unnatural warped

## pester

(verb) If you pester someone, you keep bothering them or asking them to do something.

e.g. *The kids have been pestering me to buy them new trainers.*

    badger bother get at harass hassle importune nag plague torment worry

## picture

(noun) A picture of someone or something is a drawing, painting, or photograph of them.

e.g. *a big picture on the front page.*

figure   illustration   impression   likeness   sketch

## pierce

(verb) If a sharp object pierces something, it goes through it, making a hole.

e.g. *artillery powerful enough to pierce an armoured vehicle.*

penetrate   perforate   prick   puncture   stab   transfix

## piercing

(adjective) A piercing sound is high-pitched, sharp, and unpleasant.

e.g. *She let out a piercing wail.*

ear-splitting   excruciating   high-pitched
penetrating   sharp   shrill

## pity

**1.** (verb) If you pity someone, you feel very sorry for them.

e.g. *I pity the poor man she marries.*

commiserate with   feel for   feel sorry for   grieve for
have compassion for   sympathize with

**2.** (noun) Pity is a feeling of being sorry for someone.

e.g. *He felt, instead, a flash of pity and a desire to put things right.*

commiseration   compassion   fellow feeling
sympathy

## place

(noun) A place is any point, building, or area.

e.g. *a public place.*

area   location   point   position   site   situation   spot
whereabouts

## placid

(adjective) calm and not easily excited or upset.

e.g. *Labradors are usually placid dogs.*

calm   equable   even-tempered   phlegmatic
tranquil   unruffled

## plain .

**1.** (adjective) very simple in style with no pattern or
decoration.

e.g. *plain walls.*

austere   bare   basic   natural   restrained   severe
simple   stark   unadorned

**2.** obvious and easy to understand or recognize.

e.g. *The facts are plain enough.*

apparent   clear   comprehensible   distinct   evident
manifest   obvious   patent   transparent
unambiguous   unmistakable   visible

## plan

**1.** (noun) A plan is a method of achieving something
that has been worked out beforehand.

e.g. *a long-term plan of action.*

blueprint   design   formula   idea   method   policy
procedure   ruse   scheme   strategy   system

**2.** (verb) If you plan something, you decide in detail
what it is to be and how to do it.

e.g. *Plan your menu well in advance.*

arrange design devise draft formulate organize

**3.** If you are planning to do something, you intend to do it.

e.g. *They plan to marry in the summer.*

aim intend mean propose

# pleasant

(adjective) enjoyable, likable, or attractive.

e.g. *a pleasant personality.*

agreeable amiable charming congenial delectable delightful engaging enjoyable good gracious gratifying likable nice personable pleasing pleasurable

# please

(verb) If something pleases you, it makes you feel happy and satisfied.

e.g. *He's very easy to please.*

cheer content delight gladden gratify satisfy suit tickle

# pliable

(adjective) If something is pliable, you can bend it without breaking it.

e.g. *pliable stems.*

ductile elastic flexible malleable plastic pliant supple

# plot

**1.** (noun) A plot is a secret plan made by a group of people.

e.g. *the potential victim of some plot.*

conspiracy   intrigue   stratagem   subterfuge

**2.** (verb) If people plot to do something, they plan it secretly.

e.g. *His family is plotting to disinherit him.*

conspire   manoeuvre   scheme

## plump

(adjective) rather fat.

e.g. *a small plump baby.*

buxom   chubby   dumpy   podgy   portly   roly-poly
stout   tubby

## plunge

(verb) If something plunges, it falls suddenly.

e.g. *He plunged into the cold sea.*

dive   drop   fall   pitch   plummet   sink   swoop

## poison

(noun) Poison is a substance that can kill people or animals if they swallow it or absorb it.

e.g. *He tried to kill his wife with rat poison.*

toxin   venom

## poke

(verb) If you poke someone or something, you push at them quickly with your finger or a sharp object.

e.g. *He poked me in the eye with his finger.*

dig   jab   prod   stab

## polish

(verb) If you polish something, you put polish on it or rub it with a cloth to make it shine.

e.g. *Every Sunday he polishes his car.*

buff  burnish  rub  shine  wax

## polite

(adjective) Someone who is polite has good manners and behaves considerately towards other people.

e.g. *It doesn't cost anything to be polite.*

civil  courteous  gracious  respectful  well-behaved  well-mannered

## pollute

(verb) To pollute water or air means to make it dirty and dangerous to use or live in.

e.g. *These gases pollute the atmosphere.*

contaminate  dirty  foul  infect  mar  poison  sully  taint

## ponder

(verb) If you ponder, you think about something deeply.

e.g. *He was pondering the problem when Phillipson drove up.*

brood over  cogitate  contemplate  deliberate  meditate  mull over  muse  reflect  ruminate

## pontificate

(verb) If someone pontificates, they state their opinions as if they are obviously correct.

e.g. *He loves to pontificate on things he knows nothing about.*

expound  hold forth  lay down the law

## poor

(adjective) Poor people have very little money and few possessions.

e.g. *She came from a very poor family.*

destitute  impecunious  impoverished  needy
penniless  penurious  poverty-stricken

## popular

(adjective) enjoyed, approved of, or liked by a lot of
people.

e.g. *a very popular family car.*

fashionable  favourite  in  in favour  prevailing
well-liked

## portion

(noun) A portion of something is a part or amount of
it.

e.g. *a portion of fresh fruit.*

helping  piece  share

## pose

(noun) A pose is the way someone is sitting, standing,
or lying.

e.g. *hundreds of photographs in various poses.*

attitude  position  posture  stance

## positive

(adjective) providing definite proof of the truth or
identity of something.

e.g. *positive evidence.*

affirmative  categorical  certain  clear-cut
conclusive  concrete  decisive  definite  explicit
firm  unmistakable

## possession

(noun) Your possessions are the things that you own
or that you have with you.

e.g. *I came home to find Billy rooting through my possessions.*

   assets belongings chattels effects property things

## possibility

(noun) A possibility is something that might be true or might happen.

e.g. *the possibility of a ban.*

   chance hope likelihood prospect

## possible

(adjective) likely to happen or able to be done.

e.g. *They want to raise as much money for charity as possible.*

   conceivable feasible potential practicable

## postpone

(verb) If you postpone an event, you arrange for it to take place at a later time than was originally planned.

e.g. *We'll have to postpone our meeting.*

   adjourn defer procrastinate put off shelve

## potential

(adjective) capable of becoming the kind of thing mentioned.

e.g. *potential sources of finance.*

   dormant future latent likely possible unrealized

## pour

(verb) When it is raining heavily, you can say that it is pouring.

e.g. *It was the rush hour and pouring with rain.*

bucket  pelt  teem

## poverty

(noun) Poverty is the state of being very poor.

e.g. *conditions of dire poverty.*

destitution  need  penury  privation  want

## power

(noun) The power of something is the physical strength that it has to move things.

e.g. *The car handled nicely but lacked power.*

energy  force  potency  strength

## powerless

(adjective) unable to control or influence events.

e.g. *She was powerless to save her son.*

helpless  impotent  incapable

## practical

(adjective) Ideas, methods, tools, or clothes that are practical are sensible and likely to be effective.

e.g. *practical low-heeled shoes.*

businesslike  down-to-earth  functional  pragmatic
realistic  sensible  utilitarian

## praise

**1.** (verb) If you praise someone or something, you express strong approval of their qualities or achievements.

e.g. *It is important to praise children when they do well.*

acclaim  applaud  commend  compliment
congratulate  eulogize  extol

**2.** (noun) Praise is what is said or written in approval

of someone's qualities or achievements.

e.g. *I don't deserve half of your generous praise.*

    acclamation accolade applause approval
commendation compliment congratulation
eulogy tribute

## precarious

**1.** (adjective) If your situation is precarious, you may
fail in what you are doing at any time.

e.g. *Advertising is a precarious profession.*

    dangerous dicey *informal* dodgy *informal* doubtful
hairy *informal* hazardous risky uncertain

**2.** Something that is precarious is likely to fall
because it is not well balanced or secured.

e.g. *precarious-looking iron bridges.*

    insecure shaky unsafe unstable unsteady

## precaution

(noun) A precaution is an action that is intended to
prevent something from happening.

e.g. *It's still worth taking precautions against accidents.*

    insurance safeguard safety measure

## predicament

(noun) If you are in a predicament, you are in a
difficult situation.

e.g. *the hopelessness of her predicament.*

    corner dilemma emergency fix *informal* hole
*informal* plight quandary

## predict

(verb) If someone predicts an event, they say that it

will happen in the future.

e.g. *Observers predict a glittering future for him.*

   forecast  foresee  foretell  prophesy

## predominant

(adjective) more important or more noticeable than anything else in a particular set of people or things.

e.g. *the predominant opinion in the West.*

   controlling  dominant  main  paramount
   prevailing  prevalent  principal  ruling

## preliminary

(adjective) Preliminary activities take place before something starts, in preparation for it.

e.g. *the preliminary rounds of the competition.*

   introductory  prefatory  preparatory  qualifying  trial

## premonition

(noun) A premonition is a feeling that something unpleasant is going to happen.

e.g. *a sudden premonition of disaster.*

   apprehension  foreboding  presentiment

## present

(adjective) A present situation is one that exists now rather than in the past or the future.

e.g. *How satisfied are you with your present job?.*

   contemporary  current  existing  immediate
   present-day

## prestige

(noun) If you have prestige, people admire you because of your position.

e.g. *a position of wealth and prestige.*

distinction eminence esteem renown standing
stature status

## presume

(verb) If you presume something, you think that it is
the case although you have no proof.

e.g. *I presume the vacancy will be advertised.*

assume presuppose suppose surmise

## pretend

(verb) If you pretend that something is the case, you
try to make people believe that it is, although in fact it
is not.

e.g. *Latimer pretended not to notice.*

affect bluff feign profess sham simulate

## prevent

(verb) If you prevent something, you stop it from
happening or being done.

e.g. *efforts to prevent publication.*

avert avoid balk foil forestall frustrate
preclude restrain stave off stop

## previous

(adjective) happening or existing before something
else in time or position.

e.g. *previous reports.*

earlier former old past preceding prior

## price

(noun) The price of something is the amount of
money you have to pay to buy it.

e.g. *two for the price of one.*

> amount charge cost fee figure rate

## pride

(noun) Pride is a feeling of satisfaction you have when you have done something well.

e.g. *He can look back on his efforts with pride.*

> dignity honour satisfaction self-esteem self-respect

## prim

(adjective) Someone who is prim always behaves very correctly and is easily shocked by anything rude.

e.g. *She acts like a prim maiden aunt.*

> priggish proper prudish puritanical staid strait-laced

## prime

(noun) Someone's prime is the stage when they are at their strongest, most active, or most successful.

e.g. *I'm not middle-aged, I'm in my prime.*

> best bloom height heyday

## principle

(noun) A principle is a belief you have about the way you should behave.

e.g. *I try to live according to my principles.*

> belief ethic ideal moral standard value

## prize

(noun) A prize is a reward given to the winner of a competition or game.

e.g. *the star prize in the raffle.*

award  jackpot  reward  trophy  winnings

## probability

(noun) The probability of something happening is
how likely it is to happen.

e.g. *This will greatly increase the probability of success.*

chance  expectation  likelihood  odds  prospect

## problem

(noun) A problem is an unsatisfactory situation that
causes difficulties.

e.g. *The problem is reaching epidemic proportions.*

complication  difficulty  drawback  hitch  snag

## productive

**1.** (adjective) To be productive means to produce a
large number of things.

e.g. *Farms were more productive in these areas.*

fertile  fruitful  prolific

**2.** If something such as a meeting is productive, good
or useful things happen as a result of it.

e.g. *a long and productive life.*

fruitful  profitable  rewarding  useful  worthwhile

## profit

(noun) When someone sells something, the profit is
the amount they gain by selling it for more than it
cost them to buy or make.

e.g. *We split the profit between us.*

earnings  gains  proceeds  receipts  returns
revenue  takings

## programme

(noun) You can refer to a planned series of events as a programme.

e.g. *her packed programme of official engagements.*

agenda course curriculum schedule syllabus timetable

## progress

**1.** (noun) Progress is the process of gradually improving or getting near to achieving something.

e.g. *They made good progress.*

advance development headway improvement

**2.** The progress of something is the way in which it develops or continues.

e.g. *news on the progress of the war.*

course development movement progression

## promiscuous

(adjective) Someone who is promiscuous has sex with many different people.

e.g. *You don't have to be promiscuous to be at risk from AIDS.*

abandoned debauched dissipated dissolute licentious loose wanton

## promise

**1.** (verb) If you promise to do something, you say that you will definitely do it.

e.g. *He would never promise something he couldn't fulfil.*

guarantee pledge swear undertake vow

**2.** (noun) A promise is a statement made by

someone that they will definitely do something.

e.g. *He made a promise to the men.*

assurance  oath  pledge  vow  word

## prone

(adjective) If you are prone to something, you have a tendency to be affected by it or to do it.

e.g. *She is prone to depression.*

disposed  given  inclined  liable  predisposed
subject  susceptible

## proof

(noun) If you have proof of something, you have evidence which shows that it happened, is true, or exists.

e.g. *Here's proof that this idea works.*

authentication  confirmation  corroboration
evidence  substantiation  verification

## prospect

(noun) Someone's prospects are their chances of being successful in the future.

e.g. *I wanted to further my career prospects.*

expectation  future  outlook

## proud

(adjective) having great dignity and self-respect.

e.g. *He was too proud to ask his family for help.*

arrogant  conceited  haughty  high and mighty
*informal*  self-important  snooty *informal*  stuck-up
*informal*

## prove

(verb) To prove that something is true means to provide evidence that it is definitely true.

e.g. *A letter from Nora proved that he lived there.*

authenticate  confirm  corroborate  demonstrate  establish  show  substantiate  verify

## provide

(verb) If you provide something for someone, you give it to them or make it available for them.

e.g. *a network of friends who can provide help and support.*

cater for  equip  furnish  lay on  purvey  stock up  supply

## public

(adjective) provided for everyone to use, or open to anyone.

e.g. *public transport.*

civic  civil  communal  general  national  open  state  unrestricted

## punctual

(adjective) arriving at the correct time.

e.g. *He dislikes people who are not punctual.*

on time  prompt  timely

## punish

(verb) To punish someone who has done something wrong means to make them suffer because of it.

e.g. *You've got to punish the ringleaders.*

chastise  correct  discipline  penalize

## pure

**1.** (adjective) Pure means clean and free from harmful substances.

e.g. *The water is pure enough to drink.*

> clean  spotless  sterile  sterilized  unadulterated
> unpolluted  unsullied

**2.** People who are pure have not done anything considered to be sinful.

e.g. *a pure young woman of good family.*

> blameless  chaste  impeccable  innocent
> undefiled  unsullied  virginal  virtuous

## push

(verb) When you push something, you press it using force in order to move it.

e.g. *Push the table back against the wall.*

> drive  jog  jostle  poke  press  propel  ram  shove
> thrust

## put

(verb) When you put something somewhere, you move it into that place or position.

e.g. *He sat back and put his feet on the desk.*

> deposit  fix  lay  place  position  rest  set  settle

## put across

(verb) When you put something across, you make someone understand it.

e.g. *It's very hard to put across the facts.*

> communicate  convey  explain  spell out

## puzzle

(verb) If something puzzles you, it confuses you and you do not understand it.

e.g. *There was something about her that puzzled me.*

baffle bamboozle bemuse bewilder confound confuse flummox mystify perplex stump

# Q q

## quarrel

**1.** (noun) A quarrel is an angry argument.

e.g. *I had a terrible quarrel with my other brothers.*

altercation  argument  disagreement  dispute
fight  row  squabble  tiff

**2.** (verb) If people quarrel, they have an angry argument.

e.g. *The man quarrelled with the driver.*

argue  bicker  differ  disagree  dispute  fall out
fight  row  squabble  wrangle

## quarrelsome

(adjective) often quarrelling.

e.g. *His brothers were greedy and quarrelsome.*

argumentative  contentious

## question

**1.** (noun) A question is a sentence which asks for information.

e.g. *You haven't answered my question.*

inquiry  query

**2.** (verb) If you question something, you express doubts about it.

e.g. *He never stopped questioning his own beliefs.*

challenge  dispute  query

## quiet

(adjective) Someone or something that is quiet makes very little noise or no noise at all.

e.g. *that quiet manner of his.*

> hushed  inaudible  low  silent  soft  soundless
> subdued  unobtrusive

## quote

**1.** (verb) If you quote a fact, you state it because it supports what you are saying.

e.g. *She quoted a great line from a book.*

> cite  detail  instance  name  recite

**2.** (noun) A quote is an extract from a book or speech.

e.g. *a quote from the newspaper.*

> citation  quotation

# *R r*

## rage

(verb) To rage about something means to speak angrily about it.

e.g. *He raged about the unfairness of this.*

fume rant rave seethe storm

## rampage

(verb) To rampage means to rush about wildly causing damage.

e.g. *Within minutes the mob was rampaging through the streets.*

go berserk rage run amuck run riot storm

## ramshackle

(adjective) A ramshackle building is in poor condition, and likely to fall down.

e.g. *a ramshackle old tractor shed.*

crumbling decrepit derelict dilapidated rickety tumbledown

## random

(adjective) A random choice or arrangement is not based on any definite plan.

e.g. *a random sample of local residents.*

arbitrary chance fortuitous haphazard unplanned

## range

(noun) A range is a number of different things of the same kind.

e.g. *A wide range of colours are available.*

extent gamut scope spectrum sweep variety

## rapport

(noun; a formal word) If there is a rapport between two people, they find it easy to understand each other's feelings and attitudes.

e.g. *The emotional rapport between mother and child.*

affinity bond empathy harmony sympathy understanding

## rash

(adjective) If you are rash, you do something hasty and foolish.

e.g. *It would be a rash pundit who would bet against him.*

foolhardy hasty heedless hot-headed ill-advised impetuous imprudent impulsive incautious irresponsible reckless

## rather

**1.** (adverb) Rather means to a certain extent.

e.g. *The reality is rather complex.*

fairly moderately quite relatively slightly somewhat

**2.** If you would rather do a particular thing, you would prefer to do it.

e.g. *I would rather stay here.*

preferably sooner

### ratio

(noun) A ratio is a relationship which shows how many times one thing is bigger than another.

e.g. *The adult to child ratio is 1 to 6.*

    proportion  rate  relation

### reaction

**1.** (noun) Your reaction to something is what you feel, say, or do because of it.

e.g. *Reaction to the visit is mixed.*

    feedback  response

**2.** If there is a reaction against something, it becomes unpopular.

e.g. *a reaction against Christianity.*

    backlash

### real

(adjective) genuine and not imitation.

e.g. *Who's to know if they're real guns?.*

    actual  authentic  genuine  original

### reality

(noun) Reality is the real nature of things, rather than the way someone imagines it.

e.g. *Fiction and reality were increasingly blurred.*

    actuality  fact  facts  truth

### reason

**1.** (noun) The reason for something is the fact or situation which explains why it happens or which causes it to happen.

e.g. *Most women cite self-defence as their reason for*

*carrying a gun.*

> cause   grounds   motive

**2.** Reason is the ability to think and make judgments.

e.g. *He lost all sense of reason.*

> intellect   judgment   logic   sense   understanding

## rebellion

(noun) A rebellion is organized and often violent opposition to authority.

e.g. *a ferocious rebellion against Russian settlers.*

> insurrection   mutiny   resistance   revolt   revolution
> uprising

## recession

(noun) A recession is a period when a country's economy is less successful and more people become unemployed.

e.g. *The recession has damaged the chances of disabled people obtaining work.*

> decline   depression   downturn   slump

## recognize

(verb) If you recognize someone or something, you realize that you know who or what they are.

e.g. *The receptionist recognized me at once.*

> identify   know   place   remember

## reconstruct

**1.** (verb) To reconstruct something that has been damaged means to build it again.

e.g. *The dilapidated house was to have been reconstructed brick by brick.*

rebuild   renovate   restore

**2.** To reconstruct a past event means to obtain a complete description of it from small pieces of information.

e.g. *Hutchinson later reconstructed the alleged murder for police.*

build up   recreate   regenerate

# record

**1.** (noun) If you keep a record of something, you keep a written account or store information in a computer.

e.g. *medical records.*

annals   archive   chronicle   file   history   minutes

**2.** (verb) If you record information, you write it down or put it into a computer.

e.g. *The coroner recorded a verdict of accidental death.*

enter   file   log   minute   register   report   transcribe

# recover

**1.** (verb) To recover from an illness or unhappy experience means to get well again or get over it.

e.g. *He was recovering from a serious head injury.*

convalesce   heal   improve   mend   rally
recuperate   revive

**2.** If you recover a lost object or your ability to do something, you get it back.

e.g. *Harry recovered his sense of humour.*

make good   reclaim   recoup   regain   repossess
retrieve

## reduce

(verb) To reduce something means to make it smaller in size or amount.

e.g. *Cuts have severely reduced the number of schools with their own orchestras.*

compress condense curtail cut decrease
diminish dock lessen lower narrow pare
shorten trim

## refined

(adjective) very polite and well-mannered.

e.g. *Football is meant to be a refined and cultured art.*

civilized cultivated cultured genteel ladylike
polished polite urbane

## reform

(verb) When people reform, they stop committing crimes or doing other unacceptable things.

e.g. *When his first court case was coming up, James promised to reform.*

go straight mend your ways turn over a new leaf

## refresh

(verb) If something refreshes you when you are hot or tired, it makes you feel cooler or more energetic.

e.g. *a refreshing glass of fruit juice.*

freshen invigorate revitalize revive stimulate

## refuge

(noun) A refuge is a place where you go for safety.

e.g. *The pink-walled cottage was his refuge from the bustle of London.*

asylum haven retreat sanctuary shelter

## refund

(verb) To refund someone's money means to return it to them after they have paid for something with it.

e.g. *The seller of the dog is legally bound to refund your money.*

pay back   reimburse   repay

## region

(noun) A region is a large area of land.

e.g. *He went to live in a remote region of Spain.*

area   district   expanse   province   sector   territory zone

## regret

(verb) If you regret something, you are sorry that it happened.

e.g. *I do regret not having had a proper education.*

bemoan   deplore   mourn   repent   rue

## regular

(adjective) even and equally spaced.

e.g. *soft music with a regular beat.*

consistent   constant   even   fixed   set   steady symmetrical   uniform

## reject

**1.** (verb) If you reject a proposal or request, you do not accept it or agree to it.

e.g. *The Rugby League rejected their appeal for compensation.*

decline   rebuff   refuse   repudiate   turn down

**2.** If you reject a belief, political system, or way of

life, you decide that it is not for you.

e.g. *Some adolescents reject the lifestyle of the older generation.*

discard renounce repudiate shun spurn

## relation

(noun) If there is a relation between two things, they are similar or connected in some way.

e.g. *This theory bears no relation to reality.*

comparison connection correspondence
relationship similarity

## relax

**1.** (verb) If you relax, you become calm and your muscles lose their tension.

e.g. *We can all relax over coffee and biscuits.*

loosen up rest unwind

**2.** If you relax your hold, you hold something less tightly.

e.g. *The German relaxed his grip on the steering wheel.*

ease loose loosen slacken weaken

## relegate

(verb) To relegate something or someone means to give them a less important position or status.

e.g. *He was relegated to the role of spectator.*

demote downgrade

## relentless

(adjective) never stopping and never reducing in severity.

e.g. *the relentless rise of business closures.*

> pitiless remorseless uncompromising unrelenting
> unyielding

## relevant

(adjective) If something is relevant, it is connected
with and is appropriate to what is being discussed.

e.g. *We have passed all relevant information on to the
police.*

> applicable apposite appropriate germane
> pertinent related

## religion

(noun) A religion is a system of religious belief.

e.g. *Every religion has elements that can offend people of
a different faith.*

> creed cult sect

## religious

(adjective) Someone who is religious has a strong
belief in a god or gods.

e.g. *A kind-hearted and deeply religious woman.*

> devout godly pious

## remains

(plural noun) The remains of something are the parts
that are left after most of it has been destroyed.

e.g. *the remains of an ancient mosque.*

> debris remnants traces vestiges

## remark

**1.** (verb) If you remark on something, you mention it
or comment on it.

e.g. *On several occasions she had remarked on the boy's
improvement.*

comment   mention

**2.** (noun) A remark is something you say, often in a casual way.

e.g. *He made some banal remark about the lateness of the spring.*

comment   observation   utterance

## remarkable

(adjective) impressive and unexpected.

e.g. *It was a remarkable achievement.*

impressive   notable   noteworthy   outstanding
phenomenal   significant   singular   striking
uncommon   wonderful

## remember

(verb) If you can remember someone or something from the past, you can bring them into your mind or think about them.

e.g. *I can still remember the headlines on the newspaper placards.*

commemorate   recall   recognize   recollect
reminisce

## remorse

(noun; a formal word) Remorse is a strong feeling of guilt.

e.g. *Keith spent the night in sleepless remorse at what he had done.*

compunction   contrition   penitence   regret
repentance   self-reproach

## remove

(verb) If you remove something from a place, you take it off or away.

e.g. *He removed the stereo from his brother's car.*

    detach efface eject eliminate extract obviate oust purge weed out withdraw

## repel

(verb) When soldiers repel an attacking force, they successfully defend themselves against it.

e.g. *Desperate operations to repel the Japanese invasion of New Guinea.*

    parry repulse resist ward off

## replace

(verb) When one thing replaces another, the first thing takes the place of the second.

e.g. *John Roberts yesterday replaced Jeremy Beasley as chairman.*

    oust succeed supersede supplant

## reply

**1.** (verb) If you reply to something, you say or write an answer.

e.g. *a polite refusal to reply.*

    answer respond retaliate retort return riposte write back

**2.** (noun) A reply is what you say or write when you answer someone.

e.g. *They never received a reply.*

    answer comeback *informal* rejoinder response retort return riposte

## report

(noun) A report is an account of an event, a situation, or a person's progress.

e.g. *Your report about banking errors was most enlightening.*

> account article description piece statement
> story write-up

## represent

(verb) To represent something in a particular way means to describe it in that way.

e.g. *The popular press tends to represent him as a hero.*

> depict describe portray render show

## representation

(noun) You can describe a picture or statue of someone as a representation of them.

e.g. *The photograph was not an accurate representation of the star.*

> likeness portrait portrayal profile

## reputation

(noun) The reputation of something or someone is the opinion that people have of them.

e.g. *The college had a good reputation.*

> character honour name repute standing

## request

(noun) If you make a request for something, you ask for it politely and formally.

e.g. *She turned down my request for an interview.*

> appeal application entreaty petition

## resemblance

(noun) If there is a resemblance between two things, they are similar to each other.

e.g. *There was a remarkable resemblance between him and Pete.*

correspondence  likeness  similarity

## reserve

(verb) If something is reserved for a particular person or purpose, it is kept specially for them.

e.g. *a wing of the prison reserved for foreigners.*

book  earmark  keep  preserve  save  set aside

## resist

(verb) If you resist something, you refuse to accept it and try to prevent it.

e.g. *The pay squeeze will be fiercely resisted by the unions.*

combat  dispute  oppose  withstand

## resonant

(adjective) A resonant sound is deep and strong.

e.g. *His voice was resonant and beautifully cultured.*

echoing  full  resounding  reverberating  rich  sonorous

## respectable

**1.** (adjective) considered to be acceptable and morally correct.

e.g. *the veneer of respectable society.*

decent  decorous  honourable  proper  reputable  respected  upright  worthy

**2.** adequate or reasonable.

e.g. *a respectable final score.*

adequate  ample  appreciable  considerable
decent  fair  presentable  reasonable  substantial

## responsibility

(noun) If you accept responsibility for something that has happened, you agree that you caused it or were to blame.

e.g. *They refuse to accept responsibility for the children.*

blame  liability  obligation  onus

## responsible

(adjective) If you are responsible for something, it is your duty to deal with it and you are to blame if it goes wrong.

e.g. *The airline was responsible for the safety of the passengers.*

accountable  answerable  liable

## rest

(noun) If you have a rest, you sit or lie quietly and relax.

e.g. *He had gone on the trip with his wife for a well-earned rest.*

break  breather  lull  respite  stop  time off

## restless

(adjective) finding it difficult to remain still or relaxed as a result of boredom or impatience.

e.g. *bored and restless youths.*

agitated  disturbed  edgy  fidgety  jumpy  restive
uneasy  unsettled

## restore

(verb) To restore an old building or work of art means to clean and repair it.

e.g. *She restored the old fort and made it into her private temple.*

do up   refurbish   renovate   retouch

## restrain

(verb) To restrain someone or something means to hold them back or prevent them from doing what they want to.

e.g. *Manning had to be restrained from leaping overboard.*

check   contain   control   curb   hold back   inhibit
suppress

## restrict

(verb) To restrict people or animals means to limit their movement or actions.

e.g. *Visibility may be restricted by fog.*

confine   cramp   hem in   impede   inhibit   limit
restrain

## restriction

(noun) A restriction is a rule or situation that limits what you can do.

e.g. *financial restrictions.*

check   condition   constraint   control   limitation
restraint

## result

(noun) The result of something is the situation that is caused by it.

e.g. *As a result of the incident he got a two-year suspension.*

aftereffect aftermath consequence effect outcome repercussion upshot

## retract

(verb) If you retract something you have said, you say that you did not mean it.

e.g. *He retracted his confession.*

recant renege repudiate revoke take back withdraw

## reveal

(verb) To reveal something means to tell people about it.

e.g. *They were not ready to reveal any of the details.*

disclose divulge impart leak let slip publish tell unfold unveil

## revel

(verb) If you revel in a situation, you enjoy it very much.

e.g. *She revelled in her stardom.*

delight luxuriate relish savour thrive on wallow

## revenge

**1.** (noun) Revenge involves hurting someone who has hurt you.

e.g. *She wanted to get her revenge on her brother.*

reprisal retaliation retribution vengeance

**2.** (verb) If you revenge yourself on someone who has hurt you, you hurt them in return.

e.g. *Nothing gave her greater pleasure than revenging herself on Buxton.*

avenge   even the score   retaliate   vindicate

## review

**1.** (noun) When there is a review of a situation or system, it is examined to decide whether changes are needed.

e.g. *an impartial review of education in Birmingham.*

evaluation   examination   reassessment

**2.** (verb) To review something means to examine it to decide whether changes are needed.

e.g. *The cabinet will meet this morning to review its economic policy.*

evaluate   reassess   reconsider   rethink   revise

## rhythm

(noun) Rhythm is a regular movement or beat.

e.g. *He heard the rhythm of Markham's breathing change.*

beat   cadence   metre   pulse   tempo   time

## rich

(adjective) Someone who is rich has a lot of money and possessions.

e.g. *lifestyles of the rich and famous.*

affluent   loaded *informal*   prosperous   wealthy
well-heeled *slang*   well-off   well-to-do

## rid

(verb; a formal use) To rid a place of something unpleasant means to succeed in removing it.

e.g. *the campaign to rid football of racism.*

clear free purge relieve unburden

## riddle

(noun) Something that is a riddle puzzles and confuses you.

e.g. *Scientists claimed to have solved the riddle of the birth of the Universe.*

conundrum enigma mystery poser puzzle

## right

**1.** (adjective) The right choice, action, or decision is the best or most suitable one.

e.g. *I feel sure this is the right thing to do.*

equitable ethical fair fitting just proper suitable

**2.** (noun) If you have a right to do something, you are morally or legally entitled to do it.

e.g. *You have the right to appeal against the decision.*

claim licence prerogative privilege

## rigid

(adjective) Rigid laws or systems cannot be changed and are considered severe.

e.g. *Examiners were supplied with a rigid marking scheme.*

inflexible rigorous strict unalterable uncompromising unyielding

## ring

**1.** (verb) When a bell rings, it makes a clear, loud sound.

e.g. *The phone was ringing when I got home.*
  chime  clang  knell  peal  toll

**2.** (noun) A ring is a small circle of metal worn on your finger.

e.g. *a wedding ring.*
  band  circle  hoop

## rise

(verb) If something rises, it moves upwards.

e.g. *Smoke rises up from the odd cottage chimney.*
  ascend  climb  lift  mount  soar

## risk

**1.** (noun) A risk is a chance that something unpleasant or dangerous might happen.

e.g. *the risk of a heart attack.*
  chance  danger  gamble

**2.** (verb) If you risk something unpleasant, you do something knowing that the unpleasant thing might happen as a result.

e.g. *If he doesn't play, he risks losing his place in the team.*
  chance  endanger  gamble  hazard  imperil
  jeopardize  venture

## rival

(noun) Your rival is the person you are competing with.

e.g. *He has come up against a worthy rival.*
  adversary  challenger  competitor  contender
  opponent

## rivalry

(noun) Rivalry is active competition between people.

e.g. *An intense rivalry has broken out between teenage computer wizards.*

competition   conflict   contention   opposition

## romantic

**1.** (adjective) connected with sexual love.

e.g. *a burst of romantic passion.*

amorous   lovey-dovey   loving   mushy *informal* passionate   sentimental   sloppy *informal*   soppy *British informal*

**2.** A romantic person has ideas that are not realistic, for example about love or about ways of changing society.

e.g. *the romantic ideal of bringing peace and unity to a divided country.*

dreamy   high-flown   idealistic   impractical   starry-eyed   unrealistic

## rot

**1.** (verb) When food or wood rots, it decays and can no longer be used.

e.g. *The wooden huts on the site were rotting and leaking.*

decay   decompose   deteriorate   moulder   perish putrefy

**2.** (noun) Rot is the condition that affects things when they rot.

e.g. *The timber frame was not protected against rot.*

blight   canker   decay   mould

## rotten

**1.** (adjective) decayed and no longer of use.

e.g. *The room smelled of fried onions, rotten fruit, and burned cooking oil.*

> bad corrupt decayed decaying decomposed decomposing disintegrating mouldering mouldy perished putrescent putrid

**2.** (an informal use) of very poor quality.

e.g. *She was a rotten driver.*

> awful bad deplorable dreadful lousy terrible

## rough

**1.** (adjective) uneven and not smooth.

e.g. *the rough surface of the stone.*

> broken bumpy craggy irregular jagged rocky stony uneven

**2.** showing the main features but not the details.

e.g. *a rough sketch.*

> approximate basic crude cursory hasty imperfect incomplete quick rudimentary shapeless sketchy

**3.** without enough care or gentleness.

e.g. *complaints of rough handling.*

> harsh loutish nasty rowdy severe sharp tough violent

**4.** If the sea is rough, there are large waves because of bad weather.

e.g. *a rough Channel crossing.*

> choppy squally stormy turbulent

## round

(adjective) Something round is shaped like a ball or a circle.

e.g. *a round hole in the floor.*

> circular curved cylindrical globular rotund rounded spherical

## row

(noun) A row of people or things is several of them arranged in a line.

e.g. *a row of houses.*

> bank column file line queue rank sequence tier

## rowdy

(adjective) rough and noisy.

e.g. *a gang of rowdy youths.*

> disorderly noisy obstreperous rough stroppy *informal* unruly uproarious

## royal

(adjective) belonging to or involving a queen, a king, or a member of their family.

e.g. *They built a royal palace for their king.*

> august imperial princely queenly regal sovereign

## rubbish

**1.** (noun) Rubbish is unwanted things or waste material.

e.g. *a filthy campsite covered in rubbish.*

> debris garbage junk litter refuse trash waste

**2.** You can refer to nonsense or something of very poor quality as rubbish.

e.g. *Ferguson dismissed the claims as rubbish.*

    drivel gibberish nonsense piffle *informal* rot
    trash twaddle

## rude

(adjective) not polite.

e.g. *rude remarks about politicians.*

    abusive discourteous impolite insolent insulting
    offhand uncivil unmannerly

## rule

(noun) Rules are statements which tell you what you are allowed to do.

e.g. *the rules of grammar.*

    axiom direction guideline law maxim order
    ordinance precept principle regulation standard

## rumour

(noun) A rumour is a story that people are talking about, which may or may not be true.

e.g. *There was a rumour that two policemen had been shot.*

    gossip hearsay report story whisper word

## run

**1.** (verb) When you run, you move quickly, leaving the ground during each stride.

e.g. *I whooped for joy and ran across the lawn shouting.*

    bolt career dart dash gallop hare hasten
    hurry jog race rush scamper scramble scurry
    speed sprint

**2.** If you run away from a place, you leave it suddenly and secretly.

e.g. *He ran away from his school.*

   abscond  bolt  decamp  escape  flee  go

## runaway

(noun) A runaway is a person who has escaped from a place or left it secretly and hurriedly.

e.g. *They battled for three hours to catch the runaways.*

   deserter  escapee  fugitive  truant

## rural

(adjective) relating to or involving the countryside.

e.g. *a deeply felt nostalgia for rural life.*

   country  pastoral  rustic

# _S s_

## sack

(verb; an informal use) If someone is sacked, they are dismissed from their job by their employer.

e.g. _the tearful face of the maid she'd sacked for theft._

discharge dismiss fire

## sacrifice

(verb) If you sacrifice something valuable or important, you give it up.

e.g. _sacrificing the interests of a British company in favour of an American deal._

forego forfeit give up

## sad

(adjective) If you are sad, you feel unhappy.

e.g. _I hated it when I left and saw her looking sad._

down in the dumps gloomy melancholy miserable mournful pensive unhappy

## safe

(adjective) If you are safe, you are not in any danger.

e.g. _They will bring you to a safe place where you can spend the next two or three days._

safe and sound secure unharmed unhurt unscathed

## salvation

(noun) When someone's salvation takes place, they are saved from harm or evil.

e.g. *Burgoyne's troops were now beyond salvation.*

deliverance escape redemption rescue saving

## satisfy

(verb) To satisfy someone means to give them enough of something to make them pleased or contented.

e.g. *compromises designed to satisfy everyone but failing to please anyone.*

answer appease assuage content gratify indulge

## satisfying

(adjective) Something that is satisfying gives you a feeling of pleasure and fulfilment.

e.g. *the most satisfying moment of his whole career.*

enriching fulfilling gratifying pleasing rewarding satisfactory

## savage

(adjective) cruel and violent.

e.g. *savage fighting.*

barbarous bloodthirsty brutal cruel ferocious murderous uncivilized vicious

## save

(verb) If you save someone, you rescue them or help to keep them safe.

e.g. *He saved a whole family during the blitz.*

deliver free liberate redeem rescue

## say

(verb) When you say something, you speak words.

e.g. *He phoned and said I'm not to ask you any*

*questions.*

> comment declare mention remark speak state utter

## saying

(noun) A saying is a well-known sentence or phrase that tells you something about human life.

e.g. *Besides, there is a saying in England, is there not, "Why keep a dog and bark yourself?".*

> adage aphorism axiom maxim motto proverb saw

## scare

(verb) If something scares you, it frightens you.

e.g. *"Is it a warning? Are they trying to scare us?" he wondered.*

> alarm frighten shock startle terrify

## scathing

(adjective) harsh and scornful.

e.g. *They were scathing about his job.*

> caustic cutting sarcastic scornful virulent vitriolic withering

## scatter

**1.** (verb) To scatter things means to throw or drop them all over an area.

e.g. *hobbling out to scatter scraps for the hens.*

> fling litter shower sprinkle strew

**2.** If people scatter, they suddenly move away in different directions.

e.g. *like the end of a holiday when new acquaintances*

*scatter at the airport.*
> disband  disperse

## scold

(verb) If you scold someone, you tell them off.

e.g. *He never scolded or criticized them.*

> admonish  berate  castigate  chastise  chide
> lecture  rebuke  reprimand  reproach  reprove  tick
> off

## scornful

(adjective) showing contempt.

e.g. *his scornful comment.*

> contemptuous  derisive  disdainful  mocking
> sardonic  scathing  slighting  sneering  supercilious

## scream

(verb) If you scream, you shout or cry in a loud,
high-pitched voice.

e.g. *A few of the crowd screamed and ran away.*

> cry  howl  screech  shriek  yell

## scrounge

(verb; an informal word) If you scrounge something,
you get it by asking for it rather than by earning or
buying it.

e.g. *a bag of oranges scrounged from the hotel.*

> beg  cadge  sponge

## scruffy

(adjective) dirty and untidy.

e.g. *four scruffy youths.*

> disreputable  seedy  slovenly  tatty  unkempt

## search

**1.** (verb) If you search for something, you look for it in several places.

e.g. *Suppose we search the house first?*.

    check comb examine hunt look for ransack scour seek sift through

**2.** (noun) A search is an attempt to find something.

e.g. *After a long search he found it.*

    examination hunt inquiry investigation pursuit quest

## secret

(adjective) Something that is secret is told to only a small number of people and hidden from everyone else.

e.g. *a secret meeting.*

    clandestine classified confidential covert hush-hush underground

## secretive

(adjective) Secretive people tend to hide their feelings and intentions.

e.g. *Jake was very secretive about his family affairs.*

    close enigmatic furtive reticent stealthy surreptitious

## section

(noun) A section of something is one of the parts it is divided into.

e.g. *The first section of the motorway was opened in 1975.*

    instalment part portion segment

## sediment

(noun) Sediment is solid material that settles at the bottom of a liquid.

e.g. *Let the sediment created by this fermentation settle.*

    deposit  dregs  grounds  lees  residue

## see

(verb) If you see something, you are looking at it or you notice it.

e.g. *I could see Jenny in the studio.*

    catch sight of  discern  distinguish  espy  glimpse
    notice  observe  perceive  sight  spot  spy

## selection

(noun) A selection of things or people is a set of them chosen from a larger group.

e.g. *a short selection of my personal favourites.*

    assortment  collection  medley  miscellany  range
    variety

## selfish

(adjective) caring only about yourself, and not about other people.

e.g. *The ruling group placed selfish interests above those of mankind.*

    egotistic  greedy  mercenary  self-seeking
    ungenerous

## self-righteous

(adjective) convinced that you are better or more virtuous than other people.

e.g. *derided on all sides as smug, self-righteous bores.*

    complacent  priggish  sanctimonious  self-satisfied

smug superior

## sell

(verb) If a shop sells something, it has it available for people to buy.

e.g. *a tobacconist that sells stamps.*

handle market retail stock trade in

## send

(verb) If you send something to someone, you arrange for it to be delivered to them.

e.g. *Some manufacturers will send you a card to remind you.*

consign convey direct dispatch forward transmit

## sensational

(adjective) causing great excitement and interest.

e.g. *the most sensational product of the U.S. movie industry.*

amazing astounding breathtaking dramatic melodramatic shocking spectacular thrilling

## sensible

(adjective) showing good sense and judgment.

e.g. *We failed to develop a sensible policy for controlling the export of steel.*

balanced intelligent judicious level-headed logical politic practical pragmatic prudent rational realistic shrewd sound wise

## sensual

(adjective) showing or suggesting a liking for sexual pleasures.

e.g. *She has a wide, sensual mouth.*

carnal   erotic   sensuous   sultry   voluptuous

## sentimental

(adjective) feeling or expressing tenderness, romance, or sadness to an exaggerated extent.

e.g. *sentimental love stories.*

emotional   maudlin   mawkish   nostalgic   romantic
sloppy   soppy   tender   touching

## separate

**1.** (verb) To separate people or things means to cause them to be apart from each other.

e.g. *taking steps to separate myself from religious bias and bigotry.*

alienate   detach   dissociate   estrange   segregate
sever

**2.** If people or things separate, they move away from each other.

e.g. *In solution, electrovalent compounds separate into their constituent ions.*

break up   diverge   divide   part   part company   split up

## series

(noun) A series of things is a number of them coming one after the other.

e.g. *a series of loud explosions.*

chain   run   sequence   string   succession   train

## serious

**1.** (adjective) A serious problem or situation is very bad and worrying.

e.g. *I hope it turns out to be nothing serious.*

acute  critical  grave  momentous  pressing
severe  urgent  weighty  worrying

**2.** People who are serious are thoughtful, quiet, and slightly humourless.

e.g. *She has a serious, thoughtful face.*

earnest  sedate  sober  solemn  thoughtful

## service

(verb) When a machine or vehicle is serviced, it is examined, adjusted, and cleaned so that it will continue working efficiently.

e.g. *She made a mental note to have the car serviced.*

overhaul  recondition

## servile

(adjective) too eager to obey people.

e.g. *respectful of rank to a servile degree.*

fawning  grovelling  ingratiating  obsequious
smarmy  subservient  sycophantic  unctuous

## set

**1.** (verb) If you set a time, price, or level, you decide what it will be.

e.g. *preconditions set by the prime minister.*

allocate  arrange  assign  establish  fix  name
schedule  settle  specify

**2.** (adjective) Something that is set is fixed and not varying.

e.g. *a set charge.*

agreed  appointed  arranged  definite  firm  fixed

hard and fast  inflexible  prescribed  regular  rigid
settled

## shabby

(adjective) old and worn in appearance.

e.g. *a shabby overcoat.*

faded  frayed  threadbare  worn  worn-out

## shake

(verb) If something shakes, it moves from side to side
or up and down with small, quick movements.

e.g. *The plane was shaking to an uncomfortable degree.*

judder  quake  quiver  rock  shiver  shudder
sway  tremble  vibrate

## shameless

(adjective) behaving in an indecent or unacceptable
way, but showing no shame or embarrassment.

e.g. *shameless dishonesty.*

audacious  barefaced  brash  brazen  flagrant
unabashed  wanton

## shape

(noun) The shape of something is the form or pattern
of its outline, for example whether it is round or
square.

e.g. *his shape unrecognizable under layers of non-
regulation clothing.*

configuration  contours  cut  form  outline

## shapely

(adjective) A shapely woman has an attractive figure.

e.g. *an attractive, shapely lady.*

buxom  curvaceous  voluptuous

## share

(noun) A share of something is a portion of it.

e.g. *He wanted a glutton's share of the takings.*

allocation  allotment  cut  part  portion  quota
ration

## sharp

(adjective) A sharp person is quick to notice or
understand things.

e.g. *You've got to be sharp to get ahead.*

acute  alert  astute  bright  clever  keen  knowing
observant  perceptive  quick

## shining

(adjective) Shining things are very bright, usually
because they are reflecting light.

e.g. *shining stainless steel tables.*

bright  brilliant  gleaming  glistening  glowing
incandescent  phosphorescent  shimmering
sparkling

## shock

**1.** (verb) If something shocks you, it upsets you
because it is unpleasant and unexpected.

e.g. *I was shocked by his appearance.*

appal  disquiet  horrify  shake  stagger  stun

**2.** You can say that something shocks you when it
offends you because it is rude or immoral.

e.g. *She went out of her way to shock the more
conventional officers.*

    disgust  outrage  scandalize

## short

(adjective) If you are short with someone, you speak to them crossly.

e.g. *Extreme fatigue made her short with him.*

    abrupt  brusque  curt  offhand  sharp  terse

## shout

(verb) If you shout something, you say it very loudly.

e.g. *He shouted something to his brother.*

    bawl  bellow  call  cry  roar  scream  yell

## show

**1.** (verb) To show that something exists or is true means to prove it.

e.g. *The survey showed that 29 per cent would now approve the treaty.*

    demonstrate  indicate  prove  reveal  teach

**2.** If a picture shows something, it represents it.

e.g. *The painting shows supporters and crowd scenes.*

    depict  exhibit  reveal

**3.** If something shows a quality or characteristic, you can see that it has it.

e.g. *Her sketches and watercolours showed promise.*

    demonstrate  display  reveal

**4.** If you show your feelings, you let people see them.

e.g. *Savage was flustered, but too proud to show it.*

    disclose  divulge  reveal

**5.** (noun) A show of a feeling is behaviour in which

you show it.

e.g. *a show of optimism.*

demonstration  display

## showy

(adjective) large or bright and intended to impress people.

e.g. *a showy house.*

flamboyant  flashy  garish  gaudy  loud
ostentatious

## shrewd

(adjective) Someone who is shrewd is intelligent and makes good judgements.

e.g. *He was really ahead of his time, a shrewd business man.*

acute  astute  canny  discerning  keen  knowing
perceptive  perspicacious  sharp

## shy

(adjective) A shy person is nervous and uncomfortable in the company of other people.

e.g. *He was quiet, soft-spoken, a shy man.*

bashful  diffident  mousy  retiring  shrinking  timid

## sick

(adjective) If you feel sick, you feel as if you are going to vomit.

e.g. *feeling sick during the night.*

ill  indisposed  nauseated  nauseous  queasy
squeamish

## sign

**1.** (noun) A sign is a mark or symbol with a particular meaning.

e.g. *a minus sign.*

cipher device emblem figure logo mark symbol

**2.** A sign is also a gesture with a particular meaning.

e.g. *She communicated with the women by signs.*

cue gesticulation gesture indication signal

## silence

(verb) To silence someone or something means to stop them talking or making a noise.

e.g. *There was laughter again, which the corporal silenced.*

cut off deaden gag hush muffle muzzle quell quieten stifle

## silent

(adjective) If you are silent, you are not saying anything.

e.g. *She stood silent, listening.*

dumb hushed mum mute quiet soundless speechless

## silly

(adjective) foolish or childish.

e.g. *It was silly to make a fuss over seating arrangements.*

absurd asinine childish daft fatuous foolish pointless puerile ridiculous senseless stupid witless

## similarity

(noun) If there is a similarity between things, they are similar in some way.

e.g. *There was no similarity between it and the writing in the ransom note.*

affinity   closeness   correspondence   likeness
relation   resemblance

## sin

**1.** (noun) Sin is wicked and immoral behaviour.

e.g. *a snare and delusion leading towards sin.*

evil   iniquity   transgression   wickedness   wrong

**2.** (verb) To sin means to do something wicked and immoral.

e.g. *They had sinned by omission.*

err   lapse   transgress

## sincere

(adjective) If you are sincere, you say things that you really mean.

e.g. *a sincere expression of friendliness.*

genuine   guileless   heartfelt   honest   true

## situation

(noun) A situation is what is happening in a particular place at a particular time.

e.g. *the political situation.*

case   circumstances   condition   position   state of
affairs

## size

(noun) The size of something is how big or small it is.

e.g. *the size of the audience.*

dimensions magnitude measurement proportions

## skilful

(adjective) If you are skilful at something, you can do it very well.

e.g. *There are singers and skilful musicians.*

able adept adroit consummate deft dexterous expert handy masterly practised professional proficient skilled

## skill

(noun) Skill is the knowledge and ability that enables you to do something well.

e.g. *her skill as an actress.*

ability art artistry craft dexterity expertise finesse knack proficiency prowess talent

## skimp

(verb) If you skimp on a task, you do it carelessly or using less material than you should.

e.g. *Don't skimp on fabric or you'll spoil the draping effect.*

scrimp stint

## slander

(noun) Slander is something untrue and malicious said about someone.

e.g. *the spreading of evil gossip and slander.*

calumny misrepresentation slur smear vilification

## slaughter

(noun) Slaughter is the killing of many people.

e.g. *joining in an orgy of slaughter and pillage.*

bloodshed carnage extermination killing
massacre murder slaying

## sleep

(noun) If you have a sleep, you sleep for a while.

e.g. *He'll be ready for a sleep soon.*

doze forty winks *informal* kip *British slang* nap
slumber snooze *informal*

## sleepy

(adjective) tired and ready to go to sleep.

e.g. *I slept right through until six, and I still feel sleepy.*

dozy drowsy lethargic sluggish somnolent

## slender

(adjective) attractively thin and graceful.

e.g. *a slender girl with long hair.*

slim svelte willowy

## slogan

(noun) A slogan is a short, easily-remembered phrase
used in advertising or by a political party.

e.g. *badges with the slogan "A woman's right to work".*

catchphrase catchword jingle motto watchword

## slope

**1.** (noun) A slope is a flat surface that is at an angle,
so that one end is higher than the other.

e.g. *down the grass slope leading to the river.*

incline slant tilt

**2.** The slope of something is the angle at which it slopes.

e.g. *a slope of ten degrees.*

    gradient  inclination

## slow

(adjective) moving, happening, or doing something with very little speed.

e.g. *children moving in a slow circle around the room.*

    creeping  dawdling  lagging  lazy  leaden
    leisurely  loitering  measured  plodding
    ponderous  sluggish  unhurried

## sly

(adjective) A sly person is cunning and good at deceiving people.

e.g. *She was pictured as a sly manipulator.*

    artful  crafty  cunning  devious  scheming  shifty
    sneaky  underhand  wily

## small

**1.** (adjective) Small means not large in size, number, or amount.

e.g. *She began to pace round the small room.*

    diminutive  little  miniature  petite  scanty  slight

**2.** Small also means not important or significant.

e.g. *small changes.*

    insignificant  lesser  limited  minor  modest
    negligible  paltry  petty  trifling  trivial

## smell

(noun) The smell of something is a quality it has

which you perceive through your nose.

e.g. *a smell of damp wood.*

aroma   odour   perfume   scent   whiff

## smooth

**1.** (adjective) A smooth surface has no roughness in it.

e.g. *The boulders were smooth and slippery.*

even   flat   flush   glassy   horizontal   level   plain
sleek   unbroken   unwrinkled

**2.** If you say that a man is smooth, you mean that he is smart, confident, and polite in a way you find rather unpleasant.

e.g. *A very smooth fellow, he seemed to know everything that was going on.*

debonair   facile   glib   slick   suave   urbane

## snub

(noun) A snub is an insulting remark or a piece of rude behaviour.

e.g. *a deliberate snub to them.*

affront   insult   rebuff   rejection   slight

## soak

(verb) When a liquid soaks something, it makes it very wet.

e.g. *his khaki shirt soaked with sweat.*

bathe   drench   immerse   saturate   steep

## sociable

(adjective) Sociable people are friendly and enjoy talking to other people.

e.g. *Usually so outgoing and sociable, she'd grown withdrawn.*

companionable   convivial   cordial   friendly
gregarious   outgoing

## society

(noun) Society is the people in a particular country or region.

e.g. *a major problem in society.*

civilization   community   culture   general public
people

## soil

(noun) Soil is the top layer on the surface of the earth in which plants grow.

e.g. *Crops failed on this poor, sandy soil.*

earth   ground   land

## solitude

(noun) Solitude is the state of being alone.

e.g. *She enjoyed her moments of solitude before the pressures of the day began.*

isolation   loneliness   privacy   retirement   seclusion

## solve

(verb) If you solve a problem or a question, you find a solution or answer to it.

e.g. *It seemed an easy problem to solve.*

answer   clear up   crack   decipher   get to the
bottom of   resolve   unravel   work out

## sophisticated

(adjective) Sophisticated people have refined or cultured tastes or habits.

e.g. *He was sophisticated and amusing, an attentive escort.*

> cosmopolitan cultivated cultured suave urbane worldly

## sordid

(adjective) dirty, unpleasant, or depressing.

e.g. *the sordid guest house.*

> seedy sleazy squalid wretched

## sore

(adjective) If part of your body is sore, it causes you pain and discomfort.

e.g. *His hand was sore and swollen.*

> inflamed painful raw sensitive smarting tender

## sorry

(adjective) If you are sorry about something, you feel sadness, regret, or sympathy because of it.

e.g. *I was so sorry to hear about your husband.*

> apologetic contrite distressed penitent regretful remorseful repentant shamefaced

## sort

(noun) The different sorts of something are the different types of it.

e.g. *five different sorts of biscuits.*

> brand category class denomination form ilk kind make quality species style type variety

## spacious

(adjective) having or providing a lot of space.

e.g. *the spacious living room.*

capacious commodious expansive extensive
roomy sizable

## spare

(adjective) extra to what is needed.

e.g. *I have lots of spare time.*

additional emergency extra free reserve
superfluous surplus unoccupied unused

## sparkle

(verb) If something sparkles, it shines with a lot of
small, bright points of light.

e.g. *Long diamond earrings sparkled at her neck.*

flash gleam glint glisten glitter scintillate
twinkle

## speak

(verb) When you speak, you use your voice to say
words.

e.g. *She started to speak, and then stopped.*

converse discourse talk utter

## specific

**1.** (adjective) Something that is specific to a thing is
connected with that thing only.

e.g. *specific areas of difficulty.*

especial particular peculiar special

**2.** precise and exact.

e.g. *She will ask for specific answers.*

certain definite exact explicit precise
unequivocal

## spectacular

(adjective) Something spectacular is very impressive or dramatic.

e.g. *spectacular views of Snowdonia.*

breathtaking daring dazzling dramatic
magnificent sensational stunning

## spectator

(noun) A spectator is a person who is watching something.

e.g. *The team was allowed to depart to the cheers of the spectators.*

bystander eyewitness observer onlooker viewer
watcher witness

## speech

(noun) A speech is a formal talk given to an audience.

e.g. *the opportunity to make his usual conventional little speech.*

address discourse lecture oration talk

## speed

**1.** (noun) The speed of something is the rate at which it moves, travels, or happens.

e.g. *The speed can be modified.*

pace rate tempo velocity

**2.** Speed is very fast movement or travel.

e.g. *The balloon dropped earthwards with considerable speed.*

alacrity haste rapidity swiftness

## spiteful

(adjective) A spiteful person does or says nasty things to people deliberately to hurt them.

e.g. *saying spiteful things about them behind their backs.*

bitchy   catty   malevolent   malicious   mean   nasty
vicious   vindictive

## splendid

(adjective) beautiful and impressive.

e.g. *a splendid Victorian mansion.*

glorious   grand   impressive   lavish   luxurious
magnificent   sumptuous

## split

**1.** (verb) If something splits or if you split it, it divides into two or more parts.

e.g. *Split the wages between you.*

cleave   crack   divide   open   part   separate

**2.** (noun) A split between two things is a division or difference between them.

e.g. *the split between rugby league and rugby union.*

breach   break   cleft   division   estrangement   rift
rupture   schism

## spoil

**1.** (verb) If you spoil something, you prevent it from being successful or satisfactory.

e.g. *nothing to spoil the perfect day.*

damage   destroy   mar   ruin   scupper *informal*
undo   wreck

**2.** To spoil children means to give them everything

they want, with harmful effects on their character.

e.g. *Elizabeth was the one she did spoil.*

    coddle  cosset  indulge  mollycoddle  pamper  pet

## spotless

(adjective) perfectly clean.

e.g. *a spotless starched white overall.*

    immaculate  impeccable  pristine  pure

## stage

(noun) A stage is a part of a process that lasts for a period of time.

e.g. *the last stage of your studies here with us.*

    juncture  period  phase  point

## stagger

(verb) If you stagger, you walk unsteadily because you are ill or drunk.

e.g. *Caught off balance, he staggered back a pace.*

    lurch  reel  sway  totter

## stale

(adjective) Stale food or air is no longer fresh.

e.g. *a stale smoky atmosphere.*

    decayed  dry  faded  fetid  flat  fusty  musty  old
sour

## stare

(verb) If you stare at something, you look at it for a long time.

e.g. *He turned his head to stare at her.*

    gape  gawk  gaze  goggle  look  watch

## start

**I.** (verb) If something or someone starts, or you start something, the first action or the first part of something happens.

e.g. *She started a programme of aerobic dancing.*

> begin commence embark upon initiate instigate originate set up

**2.** (noun) The start of something is the point or time at which it begins.

e.g. *at the start of the campaign.*

> beginning birth commencement foundation inauguration inception opening outset

## stationary

(adjective) not moving.

e.g. *a stationary car.*

> immobile inert motionless standing static

## status

(noun) A person's status is their position and importance in society.

e.g. *their newly acquired status in the community.*

> position prestige rank rating standing

## stay

(verb) If you stay in a place, you do not move away from it.

e.g. *She stayed in bed until noon.*

> continue linger remain stop tarry wait

## steady

**1.** (adjective) Something that is steady develops gradually without interruptions.

e.g. *a steady rise in prices.*

> consistent  constant  continuous  incessant
> nonstop  persistent  regular  unbroken
> uninterrupted

**2.** firm and not shaking or wobbling.

e.g. *O'Brien held out a steady hand.*

> firm  fixed  secure  stable  sure

## steal

(verb) To steal something means to take it without permission and without intending to return it.

e.g. *I saw her steal an item of clothing.*

> filch  misappropriate  nick *informal*  pilfer  pinch
> *informal*  purloin  thieve

## steep

(adjective) A steep slope rises sharply and is difficult to go up.

e.g. *overlooking a steep descent to the river.*

> precipitous  sheer

## steer

(verb) To steer a vehicle or boat means to control it so that it goes in the right direction.

e.g. *Milton steered erratically with his left hand.*

> control  direct  guide  pilot

## sterile

(adjective) Sterile means completely clean and free from germs.

e.g. *She held a sterile pad pressed against the wound.*
antiseptic aseptic disinfected sterilized

## stilted

(adjective) formal, unnatural, and rather awkward.

e.g. *a stilted conversation about American comics.*
artificial forced laboured stiff unnatural wooden

## stimulate

(verb) To stimulate something means to encourage it to begin or develop.

e.g. *The purpose of this campaign is to stimulate discussion.*
animate arouse encourage enliven excite inspire kindle prompt provoke rouse whet

## sting

(verb) If a part of your body stings, you feel a sharp tingling pain there.

e.g. *My leg began to sting painfully.*
hurt nip smart tingle

## stink

(noun) A stink is a very unpleasant smell.

e.g. *a foul stink of burning rubber.*
pong *informal* reek stench

## stomach

(noun) Your stomach is the organ inside your body where food is digested.

e.g. *His stomach felt hollow with excitement.*
abdomen  belly  gut  tummy

## stop

**1.** (verb) If you stop doing something, you no longer do it.

e.g. *We all stopped talking.*
cease  desist  discontinue  finish  leave off  quit

**2.** To stop something means to prevent it.

e.g. *Did any of them try to stop you coming?.*
bar  block  check  frustrate  hinder  impede
prevent  restrain

## store

(noun) A store of something is a supply kept for future use.

e.g. *collecting a huge store of facts.*
accumulation  cache  fund  hoard  reserve
reservoir  stock  stockpile  supply

## story

(noun) A story is a description of imaginary people and events written or told to entertain people.

e.g. *The first story is about a soldier returning from service.*
account  anecdote  narrative  saga  tale  yarn

## strain

**1.** (verb) To strain something means to force it or use it more than is reasonable or normal.

e.g. *These increases have strained the resources of the smaller countries.*

extend  overexert  overtax  overwork  stretch  tax

**2.** To strain food means to pour away the liquid from it.

e.g. *Strain any excess liquid into a separate container.*

filter  sieve  sift

**3.** (noun) Strain is worry and nervous tension.

e.g. *Overcrowding imposes severe mental strain.*

anxiety  pressure  stress  tension

## strange

**1.** (adjective) unusual or unexpected.

e.g. *Evie always wore such strange clothes.*

abnormal  bizarre  curious  extraordinary  fantastic
freakish  funny  odd  peculiar  queer  singular
uncanny  weird  zany

**2.** not known, seen, or experienced before.

e.g. *She was alone in a strange country.*

alien  exotic  foreign  new  unfamiliar  unknown

## strength

**1.** (noun) Your strength is your physical energy and the power of your muscles.

e.g. *He was at the end of his strength.*

might  robustness  stamina  toughness

**2.** You can refer to power or influence as strength.

e.g. *The campaign against pit closures gathered strength.*

energy  force  intensity  muscle  vigour

## strengthen

(verb) To strengthen something means to give it more power, influence, or support and make it more likely to succeed.

e.g. *The attacks only served to strengthen their resolve.*
bolster brace consolidate fortify intensify reinforce stiffen support toughen

## stress

**1.** (noun) Stress is worry and nervous tension.

e.g. *Regular exercise helps combat stress.*
anxiety pressure strain tension

**2.** (verb) If you stress a point, you emphasize it and draw attention to its importance.

e.g. *He had, he stressed, been forced to attack.*
accentuate emphasize highlight underline

**3.** (noun) Stress is emphasis put on a word or part of a word when it is pronounced, making it slightly louder.

e.g. *the importance of stress and intonation.*
accent emphasis

## strict

**1.** (adjective) Someone who is strict controls other people very firmly.

e.g. *He felt that my uncle was too strict, too demanding.*
authoritarian firm rigorous severe stern

**2.** A strict rule must always be obeyed absolutely.

e.g. *strict instructions not to return before dinner.*
rigid stringent

## stroll

**1.** (verb) To stroll means to walk slowly in a relaxed way.

e.g. *He rose and strolled nonchalantly towards the door.*

    amble  promenade  saunter  walk  wander

**2.** (noun) A stroll is a slow, pleasurable walk.

e.g. *She would have liked to go for a stroll.*

    airing  constitutional  ramble  turn

## strong

**1.** (adjective) Someone who is strong has powerful muscles.

e.g. *She was small and frail looking, but deceptively strong.*

    brawny  mighty  muscular  powerful  stalwart
    stout  strapping  tough

**2.** Strong also means great in degree or intensity.

e.g. *a strong sense of responsibility.*

    acute  extreme  fierce  intense  keen  marked
    violent

## structure

(noun) The structure of something is the way it is made, built, or organized.

e.g. *the structure of American society.*

    arrangement  composition  constitution
    construction  form  formation  make-up
    organization

## strut

(verb) To strut means to walk in a stiff, proud way with your chest out and your head high.

e.g. *a truculent little man, who strutted around the deck shouting at us.*

> parade  prance  swagger

## stubborn

(adjective) Someone who is stubborn is determined not to change their opinion or course of action.

e.g. *an air of stubborn determination.*

> dogged  inflexible  intransigent  obdurate
> obstinate  persistent  pig-headed  refractory  wilful

## stuffy

(adjective) If it is stuffy in a room, there is not enough fresh air.

e.g. *The room was stuffy but clean.*

> airless  close  fusty  heavy  muggy  oppressive
> stale  stifling  sultry

## stupid

(adjective) showing lack of good judgment or intelligence and not at all sensible.

e.g. *The whole thing had been stupid and unnecessary.*

> dense *informal*  dim  dull  dumb *informal*
> indiscreet  naive  obtuse  senseless  simple  slow
> slow-witted  thick *informal*

## style

(noun) A person or place that has style is smart, elegant, and fashionable.

e.g. *She had enormous talent and style, but had had no*

*formal training.*

> chic dash elegance flair panache refinement
> smartness sophistication stylishness

## stylish

(adjective) smart, elegant, and fashionable.

e.g. *He wore a stylish, European-cut suit.*

> chic dapper fashionable polished smart urbane

## subdue

(verb) If soldiers subdue a group of people, they bring them under control by using force.

e.g. *It would be quite impossible to subdue the whole continent.*

> control overcome overpower quell repress
> suppress

## substance

(noun) Anything which is a solid, a powder, a liquid, or a paste can be referred to as a substance.

e.g. *a plate of some glutinous substance that she supposed was dessert.*

> fabric material matter stuff

## substitute

**1.** (verb) To substitute one thing for another means to use it instead of the other thing or to put it in the other thing's place.

e.g. *You can also make muffins by substituting syrup for the oil.*

> exchange replace switch

**2.** (noun) If one thing is a substitute for another, it is used instead of it or put in its place.

e.g. *an acceptable substitute for the real thing.*

> deputy equivalent replacement reserve stand-by stand-in stopgap surrogate

## succeed

(verb) To succeed means to achieve the result you intend.

e.g. *She had the will to succeed.*

> do well flourish manage prosper thrive triumph

## suffice

(verb; a formal word) If something suffices, it is enough or adequate for a purpose.

e.g. *Half an hour should suffice.*

> be sufficient do serve

## suggest

**1.** (verb) If you suggest a plan or idea to someone, you mention it as a possibility for them to consider.

e.g. *I suggested she phone the hospital.*

> advise advocate move propose recommend

**2.** If something suggests a particular thought or impression, it makes you think in that way or gives you that impression.

e.g. *Nothing you say suggests he is mentally ill.*

> imply indicate

## suggestion

(noun) A suggestion is a plan or idea that is mentioned as a possibility for someone to consider.

e.g. *He agreed readily to his father's suggestion.*

> motion plan proposal proposition

recommendation

## suggestive

(adjective) Suggestive remarks or gestures make people think about sex.

e.g. *a suggestive leer.*

indecent   indelicate   naughty   provocative   racy
ribald   risqué   rude   saucy   smutty   titillating

## suitable

(adjective) right or acceptable for a particular purpose or occasion.

e.g. *trying to think of a suitable reply.*

apposite   appropriate   apt   due   fit   fitting
opportune   proper   right   satisfactory

## summary

(noun) A summary of something is a short account of its main points.

e.g. *a summary of the information contained in the charts.*

abstract   outline   précis   recapitulation   résumé
review   rundown   synopsis

## supervise

(verb) To supervise someone means to check and direct what they are doing to make sure that they do it correctly.

e.g. *appointed to supervise the household staff.*

control   look after   oversee   preside   superintend

## supplement

(verb) To supplement something means to add something to it to improve it.

e.g. *Many village men supplemented their wages by fishing for salmon.*

augment  boost  complement  top up

## suppress

(verb) If an army or government suppresses an activity, it prevents people from doing it.

e.g. *suppressed by a massive show of military force.*

check  curb  quash  quell  repress  stamp out

## supreme

(adjective) Supreme is used to emphasize the greatness of something.

e.g. *the supreme achievement of the human race.*

chief  crowning  foremost  paramount  prime
principal  superlative  ultimate

## surpass

(verb; a formal word) To surpass someone or something means to be better than them.

e.g. *Her recital that day surpassed all her previous performances.*

eclipse  exceed  excel  outclass  outdo  outshine
outstrip  transcend

## surplus

(noun) If there is a surplus of something there is more of it than is needed.

e.g. *A labour surplus existed in backward countries.*

excess  glut  overabundance  plethora  superfluity
surfeit

## surprised

(adjective) You feel surprised when something unexpected happens.

e.g. *She took it all in her stride without appearing the least surprised or pleased.*

> amazed astonished disconcerted incredulous nonplussed startled taken aback

## surrender

**1.** (verb) To surrender means to stop fighting and agree that the other side has won.

e.g. *Neither side is prepared to surrender.*

> cede concede quit yield

**2.** (noun) Surrender is a situation in which one side in a fight agrees that the other side has won and gives in.

e.g. *They would, inexorably, be starved into surrender.*

> capitulation submission

**3.** (verb) If you surrender to a temptation or feeling, you let it take control of you.

e.g. *It was easy to surrender to the charm of the place, to bask in the rosy glow of the past.*

> capitulate give in submit succumb yield

**4.** To surrender something means to give it up to someone else.

e.g. *The gallery director surrendered his keys to the building manager.*

> forego forfeit give up relinquish resign

## surround

(verb) To surround someone or something means to be situated all around them.

e.g. *the stone wall which surrounded the pool.*

circle encircle enclose encompass envelop ring

## surroundings

(plural noun) You can refer to the area and environment around a place or person as their surroundings.

e.g. *very comfortable surroundings.*

background element environment habitat milieu neighbourhood

## survey

(verb) To survey something means to look carefully at the whole of it.

e.g. *The Duchess surveyed the room critically.*

appraise assess examine inspect look over review scan study view

## suspicion

(noun) Suspicion is the feeling of not trusting someone or the feeling that something is wrong.

e.g. *their politely worded but obvious suspicion of his story.*

distrust doubt mistrust scepticism wariness

## suspicious

(adjective) Suspicious is used to describe things that make you think that there is something wrong with a situation.

e.g. *suspicious circumstances.*

doubtful dubious fishy *informal* irregular
questionable shady suspect

## swap

(verb) To swap one thing for another means to
replace the first thing with the second.

e.g. *a pack of cigarettes which I swapped for some eggs.*

barter exchange interchange switch trade

## swarm

(verb) If a place is swarming with people, there are a
lot of people there.

e.g. *When I got there the place was swarming with police.*

abound bristle crawl seethe teem throng

## sweet

(adjective) attractive and delightful.

e.g. *a sweet little baby.*

adorable appealing beautiful charming cute
engaging winning winsome

## swerve

(verb) To swerve means to suddenly change direction
to avoid colliding with something.

e.g. *Twice he had to swerve violently to avoid potholes.*

deviate diverge sheer swing veer

## swollen

(adjective) Something that is swollen has swelled up.

e.g. *The flesh above the wound was swollen and
discoloured.*

bloated distended enlarged inflamed puffy

# symbol

(noun) A symbol is a shape, design, or idea that is used to represent something.

e.g. *The fish has long been a symbol of Christianity.*

emblem  logo  representation  sign  token

# symbolic

(adjective) Something that is symbolic has a special meaning that is considered to represent something else.

e.g. *The card is symbolic of new beginnings.*

allegorical  emblematic  figurative  metaphorical representative

# sympathy

(noun) Sympathy is kindness and understanding towards someone who is in difficulties.

e.g. *His face was cold, without sympathy.*

commiseration  compassion  condolence  pity tenderness  understanding

# system

(noun) A system is an organized way of doing or arranging something according to a fixed plan or set of rules.

e.g. *an effective system of information gathering.*

method  organization  procedure  process  routine scheme  structure

# *T t*

## tackle

(verb) If you tackle a difficult task, you start dealing with it in a determined way.

e.g. *The daughters had to tackle the household washing.*

apply yourself to  begin  deal with  get to grips with  set about  take on  undertake

## tact

(noun) Tact is the ability to see when a situation is difficult or delicate and to handle it without upsetting or offending people.

e.g. *She had made her point with the utmost tact.*

consideration  delicacy  diplomacy  discretion sensitivity  thoughtfulness

## talent

(noun) Talent is the natural ability to do something well.

e.g. *my talent for debate.*

ability  aptitude  bent  capacity  flair  genius  gift knack

## talk

1. (verb) When you talk, you say things to someone.

e.g. *As they passed I heard them talking.*

chat  chatter  converse  gossip  natter *informal* speak

2. (noun) Talk is discussion or gossip.

e.g. *When the others were there, the talk was often political.*

    chat  conversation  gossip

**3.** A talk is an informal speech.

e.g. *long and interesting talks on farming and cattle raising.*

    address  discourse  lecture  oration  speech

## talkative

(adjective) talking a lot.

e.g. *a talkative bore.*

    chatty  garrulous  long-winded  loquacious
    verbose  voluble  wordy

## task

(noun) A task is any piece of work which has to be done.

e.g. *the huge task of cleaning up.*

    assignment  chore  duty  enterprise  exercise  job
    labour  mission  undertaking  work

## taste

**1.** (verb) If food or drink tastes of something, it has that flavour.

e.g. *a red meat that tastes like beef.*

    savour  smack

**2.** (noun) If you have a taste for something, you enjoy it.

e.g. *a taste for publicity.*

    appetite  desire  fancy  fondness  inclination
    liking  partiality  penchant  relish

## tax

(noun) Tax is an amount of money that citizens have to pay to the government so that it can provide public services such as health care and education.

e.g. *I pay tax on my wages.*

    duty  excise  levy  rate  tariff  toll

## teach

**1.** (verb) If you teach someone something, you give them instructions so that they know about it or know how to do it.

e.g. *They can teach children to read.*

    coach  drill  educate  instruct  school  show  train
    tutor

**2.** If you teach someone to think or behave in a certain way, you persuade them to think or behave in that way.

e.g. *She had been taught to be tough.*

    direct  educate  instruct  school  train  tutor

## team

(noun) Any group of people who work together can be called a team.

e.g. *a team of gardeners.*

    band  body  bunch  company  crew  gang  group
    set  squad

## tear

(noun) A tear in something is a hole that has been made in it.

e.g. *a tear in the muscle above the knee.*

    hole  laceration  rip  rupture

## tell

(verb) If you tell someone something, you let them know about it.

e.g. *I told him what had happened.*

announce communicate express inform narrate notify proclaim recount relate reveal say speak state utter

## temperance

(noun) Temperance is the habit of not drinking alcohol.

e.g. *a lifetime of labour and strict temperance.*

abstemiousness abstinence

## tempt

(verb) If you tempt someone, you try to persuade them to do something by offering them something they want.

e.g. *Bargain prices tempt the shopper.*

attract draw entice invite lead on lure

## tend

(verb) If something tends to happen, it happens usually or often.

e.g. *My mind tends to wander.*

be disposed to be liable to be prone to gravitate incline lean lean towards

## tendency

(noun) A tendency is a habit, trend, or type of behaviour that happens very often.

e.g. *a tendency to be critical.*

bias disposition inclination leaning liability

penchant predilection predisposition proclivity
propensity

## tender

(adjective) Someone who is tender has gentle and
caring feelings.

e.g. *He was kindly and tender.*

affectionate caring compassionate gentle
humane kind loving sensitive sympathetic
warm

## tense

(adjective) If you are tense, you are worried and
nervous and cannot relax.

e.g. *Do you feel tense or anxious for no good reason?.*

edgy jumpy keyed up nervous overwrought
restless strained uptight wired

## texture

(noun) The texture of something is the way it feels
when you touch it.

e.g. *a smooth texture.*

consistency feel grain weave

## theft

(noun) Theft is the crime of stealing.

e.g. *non-violent crimes such as theft and burglary.*

larceny pilfering robbery stealing thieving

## theory

(noun) A theory is an idea or set of ideas that is
meant to explain something.

e.g. *Darwin's theory of evolution.*

assumption conjecture guess hypothesis speculation

## thin

(adjective) A thin person or animal has very little fat on their body.

e.g. *She was thin as a wishbone.*

bony lank lanky lean meagre scraggy scrawny skinny slender slight slim spare spindly

## thing

(noun) A thing is an object, rather than a plant, an animal, a human being, or something abstract.

e.g. *I threw a few things into a bag.*

article item object

## think

**1.** (verb) When you think about ideas or problems, you use your mind to consider them.

e.g. *Dad was thinking about going home.*

brood cogitate consider contemplate deliberate meditate mull over muse ponder reason reflect ruminate

**2.** If you think something, you have the opinion that it is true or the case.

e.g. *I think she has a secret boyfriend.*

believe consider deem feel guess *chiefly U.S.* hold imagine judge presume reckon suppose surmise

## thought

(noun) Thought is the activity of thinking.

e.g. *She was lost in thought.*

cogitation  consideration  contemplation
deliberation  meditation  musing  reflection
rumination  thinking

## thoughtful

**1.** (adjective) When someone is thoughtful, they are
quiet and serious because they are thinking about
something.

e.g. *Dennis was thoughtful, saying very little.*

contemplative  meditative  musing  pensive
reflective

**2.** A thoughtful person remembers what other people
want or need, and tries to be kind to them.

e.g. *People aren't always as thoughtful as we would like
them to be.*

attentive  caring  considerate  helpful  kind
kindly  solicitous

## threaten

(verb) If someone or something threatens a person or
thing, they are likely to harm them.

e.g. *the disease that threatens him.*

endanger  jeopardize  menace

## thrill

(noun) A thrill is a sudden feeling of great
excitement, pleasure, or fear; also any event or
experience that gives you such a feeling.

e.g. *the thrill of revenge.*

buzz *slang*  charge *slang*  kick *informal*

**throw**

(verb) When you throw something you are holding, you move your hand quickly and let it go, so that it moves through the air.

e.g. _He threw away the bottle._

> bowl cast catapult chuck fling heave hurl pitch send shy sling toss

**tidy**

**1.** (adjective) Something that is tidy is neat and arranged in an orderly way.

e.g. _Ian's room was tidy._

> methodical neat ordered orderly shipshape spick and span spruce trim uncluttered well-ordered

**2.** (verb) To tidy a place means to make it neat by putting things in their proper place.

e.g. _Brenda tidied and swept the house for me._

> clear neaten order put in order spruce up straighten

**tie**

(verb) If you tie one thing to another or tie it in a particular position, you fasten it using cord of some kind.

e.g. _Ropes were tied across each staircase._

> attach bind connect fasten join lash rope

**tight**

(adjective) stretched or pulled so as not to be slack.

e.g. _a tight cord._

> rigid stiff taut tense

## tilt

(verb) If you tilt an object or it tilts, it changes position so that one end or side is higher than the other.

e.g. *She tilted her face to look up at me.*

cant  heel  incline  lean  list  pitch  slant  slope  tip

## time

(noun) Time is what is measured in hours, days, and years.

e.g. *We have enough time to prepare ourselves well.*

interval  period  phase  space  span  spell  stretch  term

## timely

(adjective) happening at just the right time.

e.g. *Mr Tabor made a timely appearance.*

convenient  opportune  punctual  well-timed

## timid

(adjective) shy and having no courage or self-confidence.

e.g. *children who are timid and unsure of themselves.*

afraid  bashful  cowardly  diffident  faint-hearted  fearful  nervous  pusillanimous  retiring  shy  timorous

## tiny

(adjective) extremely small.

e.g. *Scalpay is a tiny island.*

diminutive  infinitesimal  Lilliputian  little  miniature  minuscule  minute  slight  small  wee

## tire

**1.** (verb) If something tires you, it makes you use a lot of energy so that you want to rest or sleep.

e.g. *Hard work tired him easily.*

    drain  exhaust  fatigue  wear out  weary

**2.** If you tire of something, you become bored with it.

e.g. *Children tire of chocolate eggs.*

    weary

## together

**1.** (adverb) If people do something together, they do it with each other.

e.g. *We all knew each other well and worked together.*

    collectively  en masse  in unison  jointly

**2.** If two things happen together, they happen at the same time.

e.g. *All B vitamins should be taken together.*

    concurrently  continuously  simultaneously

## tolerable

**1.** (adjective) able to be borne or put up with.

e.g. *The dreary music is barely tolerable.*

    acceptable  bearable  endurable

**2.** fairly satisfactory or reasonable.

e.g. *a tolerable salary.*

    acceptable  adequate  average  fair  middling
    okay *informal*

## tolerate

**1.** (verb) If you tolerate things that you do not approve of or agree with, you allow them.

e.g. *They could no longer tolerate the way he runs the club.*

> abide   accept   allow   bear   brook   condone
> permit   put up with   sanction   stand   stick

**2.** If you can tolerate something, you accept it, even though it is unsatisfactory or unpleasant.

e.g. *He cannot tolerate losing.*

> abide   accept   bear   endure   put up with   stand
> stick   stomach   suffer   swallow   take

## tomb

(noun) A tomb is a large grave for one or more corpses.

e.g. *the ornate tomb of the Charpentier family.*

> crypt   grave   mausoleum   sepulchre   vault

## tonic

(noun) You can refer to anything that makes you feel stronger or more cheerful as a tonic.

e.g. *It was a tonic just being with her.*

> boost   pick-me-up   stimulant

## tool

(noun) A tool is any hand-held instrument or piece of equipment that you use to help you do a particular kind of work.

e.g. *a cutting tool.*

> appliance   contrivance   device   gadget   implement
> instrument   machine   utensil

## top

  **1.** (noun) The top of something is its highest point, part, or surface.

  e.g. *the top of the mountain.*

  apex  crest  crown  head  height  peak  pinnacle summit  vertex  zenith

  **2.** The top of a bottle, jar, or tube is its cap or lid.

  e.g. *a milk bottle top.*

  cap  cover  lid  stopper

## torment

  (noun) A torment is something that causes extreme pain and unhappiness.

  e.g. *It's a torment to see them staring at me.*

  bane  blight  plague  scourge  torture

## toss

  (verb) If you toss something somewhere, you throw it there lightly and carelessly.

  e.g. *The crowds tossed garlands at his feet.*

  cast  chuck *informal*  fling  lob  pitch  sling  throw

## total

  (noun) A total is the number you get when you add several numbers together.

  e.g. *Last year Blackpool had a total of 17 million tourists.*

  aggregate  full amount  sum  totality  whole

## touching

  (adjective) causing feelings of sadness and sympathy.

  e.g. *a touching book.*

  affecting  moving  piteous  pitiful  poignant  sad

stirring

## tough

(adjective) A tough substance is difficult to break.

e.g. *tough plastic*.

durable firm hard resilient solid strong sturdy

## trade

**1.** (noun) Trade is the activity of buying, selling, or exchanging goods or services between people, firms, or countries.

e.g. *opportunities for trade in Eastern Europe*.

barter business commerce dealing traffic transactions

**2.** (verb) When people, firms, or countries trade, they buy, sell, or exchange goods or services.

e.g. *goods from countries we trade with*.

bargain barter deal do business peddle traffic transact

## tradition

(noun) A tradition is a custom or belief that has existed for a long time without changing.

e.g. *the British tradition of taking tea*.

convention custom habit institution ritual unwritten law

## traditional

(adjective) A traditional organization or institution is one in which older methods are used rather than modern ones.

e.g. *a traditional school*.

conservative   conventional   orthodox

## transparent

(adjective) If an object or substance is transparent, you can see through it.

e.g. *transparent clothing.*

clear   diaphanous   filmy   limpid   see-through
translucent

## transport

(verb) When goods or people are transported from one place to another, they are moved there.

e.g. *the van they had used to transport furniture.*

bear   bring   carry   convey   ferry   fetch   haul
move   shuttle   take   transfer

## trap

**1.** (verb) Someone who traps animals catches them using traps.

e.g. *There were more ways to trap a tiger than by shooting it.*

catch   corner   ensnare   net   snare   take

**2.** If you trap someone, you trick them so that they do or say something which they did not want to.

e.g. *I trapped him into marriage.*

beguile   deceive   dupe   fool   trick

## travel

(verb) To travel means to go from one place to another.

e.g. *Peter has travelled throughout the world.*

commute   go   journey   move   proceed   progress

voyage

## treacherous

(adjective) A treacherous person is likely to betray you and cannot be trusted.

e.g. *a treacherous friend.*

deceitful  disloyal  faithless  false  perfidious
traitorous  unfaithful  unreliable

## trip

(noun) A trip is a journey made to a place.

e.g. *your first trip abroad.*

excursion  expedition  jaunt  journey  outing
voyage

## trouble

**1.** (noun) Troubles are difficulties or problems.

e.g. *Solve all your money troubles.*

bother  difficulty  dilemma  hassle *informal*
misfortune  predicament  problem  woe  worry

**2.** (verb) If something troubles you, it makes you feel worried or anxious.

e.g. *It still troubles me when I get jittery.*

agitate  annoy  bother  disconcert  disquiet
distress  disturb  harass  hassle *informal*  perturb
upset  vex  worry

**3.** If you trouble someone for something, you disturb them in order to ask them for it.

e.g. *I'm sorry to trouble you again.*

bother  inconvenience  put out

**true**

(adjective) A true story or statement is based on facts and is not made up.

e.g. *Allegations that had been made in the book were true.*

accurate actual authentic bona fide correct exact factual genuine honest precise real right veracious veritable

**truth**

(noun) The truth is the facts about something, rather than things that are imagined or made up.

e.g. *I know she was telling the truth.*

accuracy actuality fact genuineness legitimacy precision reality veracity verity

**try**

**1.** (verb) To try to do something means to make an effort to do it.

e.g. *I tried to get some photos.*

aim attempt bid endeavour essay have a go *informal* have a shot *informal* have a stab *informal* make an effort seek strive struggle

**2.** (noun) A try is an attempt to do something.

e.g. *It was her first try at authorship.*

attempt bid effort endeavour essay go *informal* shot *informal* stab *informal*

**turn**

(noun) If it is your turn to do something, you have the right, chance, or duty to do it.

e.g. *It is his turn to take the stage.*

chance fling go opportunity period round shot

*informal*  spell  stint  try

## twist

**1.** (verb) When you twist something you turn one
end of it in one direction while holding the other end
or turning it in the opposite direction.

e.g. *Twist the hair around your finger.*

coil  curl  entwine  screw  swivel  wind  wring

**2.** When something twists or is twisted, it moves or
bends into a strange shape.

e.g. *His face twisted in anger.*

contort  distort  screw up  warp

## typical

(adjective) showing the most usual characteristics or
behaviour.

e.g. *He looked the typical vicar.*

average  characteristic  classic  conventional
normal  orthodox  representative  standard  stock
usual

## typify

(verb) If something typifies a situation or thing, it is
characteristic of it or a typical example of it.

e.g. *The story of Ian and Katherine is one that typifies
our times.*

characterize  embody  epitomize  exemplify
illustrate  personify

# U u

### ugly

(adjective) very unattractive in appearance.

e.g. *an ugly Victorian church in red brick.*

    hideous  unattractive  unsightly

### unbearable

(adjective) Something unbearable is so unpleasant or upsetting that you feel you cannot stand it.

e.g. *The pain was unbearable.*

    intolerable  unacceptable  unendurable

### unbelievable

**1.** (adjective) extremely great or surprising.

e.g. *unbelievable courage.*

    astonishing  fantastic  incredible  staggering

**2.** so unlikely that you cannot believe it.

e.g. *I can understand why my story must have seemed unbelievable to you.*

    impossible  improbable  preposterous  unthinkable

### uncouth

(adjective) bad-mannered and unpleasant.

e.g. *a coarse, uncouth type of person.*

    boorish  coarse  loutish  rough  unrefined  vulgar

### undeniable

(adjective) certainly true.

e.g. *It is undeniable that babies show individual*

*differences at birth.*

    incontrovertible indisputable indubitable irrefutable obvious

## undermine

(verb) To undermine an idea, feeling, or system means to make it less strong or secure.

e.g. *a campaign to undermine his authority.*

    erode sabotage sap subvert weaken

## understand

(verb) If you understand what someone says, you know what they mean.

e.g. *She could speak and understand Russian.*

    appreciate comprehend fathom follow grasp know make out perceive take in

## understandable

(adjective) If something is understandable, people think it is normal or natural.

e.g. *Her father's fears were understandable, but I was able to tell him they were groundless.*

    acceptable comprehensible excusable justifiable natural reasonable

## understanding

1. (noun) If you have an understanding of something, you have some knowledge about it.

e.g. *little understanding of children's needs.*

    appreciation awareness comprehension discernment grasp insight knowledge perception perspicacity

2. (adjective) kind and sympathetic.

e.g. *Thank you for being so understanding.*

compassionate considerate kind patient
perceptive responsive sensitive tolerant

## unimportant

(adjective) having very little significance or
importance.

e.g. *Let us know if you remember anything, however
unimportant it may seem.*

inconsequential insignificant marginal minor
negligible paltry petty slight trifling trivial
worthless

## uninhibited

(adjective) If you are uninhibited, you behave freely
and naturally and show your true feelings.

e.g. *They made him laugh out loud with uninhibited
delight.*

abandoned candid frank free informal
instinctive natural open relaxed spontaneous

## unkind

(adjective) unpleasant and rather cruel.

e.g. *It had been a thoughtless, unkind act, whatever the
reason for it.*

malicious mean nasty spiteful uncharitable

## unlucky

**1.** (adjective) Someone who is unlucky has bad luck.

e.g. *those who are unlucky enough to incur his enmity.*

hapless luckless unfortunate wretched

**2.** Something that is unlucky is thought to cause bad
luck.

e.g. *Thirteen is supposed to be an unlucky number.*

cursed doomed ill-fated inauspicious ominous

## unproductive

(adjective) not producing anything useful.

e.g. *The meadows beyond were clotted with weeds and unproductive.*

barren fruitless futile idle sterile unprofitable useless

## untidy

(adjective) not neat or well arranged.

e.g. *a respectable-looking house with a wildly untidy garden.*

chaotic disorderly higgledy-piggledy *informal* jumbled muddled topsy-turvy unkempt

## unusual

(adjective) Something that is unusual does not occur very often.

e.g. *a formidable adversary, a man of quite unusual powers.*

abnormal anomalous curious different extraordinary irregular rare remarkable singular strange surprising uncommon unexpected

## unwilling

(adjective) If you are unwilling to do something, you do not want to do it.

e.g. *unable to sleep yet unwilling to leave her bed.*

averse disinclined indisposed loath reluctant

## upkeep

(noun) The upkeep of something is the continual process and cost of keeping it in good condition.

e.g. *a significant contribution to the upkeep of the estate.*

keep  maintenance  running  subsistence

## uproar

(noun) If there is uproar or an uproar, there is a lot of shouting and noise, often because people are angry.

e.g. *Harriet's voice could be heard over all the uproar.*

babel  clamour  commotion  din  furore  hubbub  outcry  pandemonium  riot  rumpus  tumult

## upset

**1.** (adjective) unhappy or disappointed because something unpleasant has happened.

e.g. *He was still upset about the accident.*

agitated  disconcerted  dismayed  distressed  disturbed  hurt  troubled  worried

**2.** (verb) If someone upsets something such as a procedure, they cause things to go wrong.

e.g. *data that upset all previous calculations of the earth's age.*

change  disorganize  disturb  spoil

**3.** If you upset something, you turn it over or spill it accidentally.

e.g. *I accidentally bumped into a table and upset a statuette.*

capsize  knock over  overturn  spill  tip over  topple over

## urge

**1.** (noun) If you have an urge to do something, you have a strong wish to do it.

e.g. *an urge to confess.*

   compulsion desire fancy impulse itch longing wish yearning

**2.** (verb) If you urge someone to do something, you try hard to persuade them to do it.

e.g. *Ginny urged her to stay on after the funeral.*

   encourage exhort goad incite press spur on

## urgent

(adjective) needing to be dealt with as soon as possible.

e.g. *She drafted replies to the most urgent letters.*

   compelling critical crucial immediate imperative pressing

## use

**1.** (verb) If you use something, you do something with it in order to do a job or achieve something.

e.g. *May I use your phone?.*

   employ utilize

**2.** (noun) The use of something is the act of using it.

e.g. *the use of force.*

   application employment exercise operation usage utilization

## useful

(adjective) If something is useful, you can use it to do something or to help you in some way.

e.g. *Each play is preceded by a useful introduction.*
> advantageous  beneficial  effective  helpful
> practical  profitable  valuable  worthwhile

## usual

(adjective) happening, done, or used most often.

e.g. *His razor and his toothbrush are in their usual places.*
> accustomed  customary  everyday  expected
> familiar  general  habitual  normal  ordinary
> routine  standard

# $V\ v$

**vague**

(adjective) If something is vague, it is not expressed or explained clearly, or you cannot see or remember it clearly.

e.g. *vague statements.*

> dim  hazy  indefinite  indeterminate  indistinct
> nebulous  obscure  shadowy  uncertain  unclear
> unspecified  woolly

**valuable**

(adjective) Something that is valuable has great value.

e.g. *a valuable necklace.*

> costly  invaluable  precious  prized  treasured
> valued

**variety**

(noun) A variety of things is a number of different kinds of them.

e.g. *a wide variety of readers.*

> array  assortment  collection  diversity  medley
> miscellany  mixture  range

**various**

(adjective) Various means of several different types.

e.g. *trees of various sorts.*

> assorted  differing  disparate  diverse
> miscellaneous  sundry  varied

### venture

(noun) A venture is something new which involves the risk of failure or of losing money.

e.g. *a successful venture in television films.*

endeavour enterprise project speculation undertaking

### verdict

**1.** (noun) In a law court, a verdict is the decision which states whether a prisoner is guilty or not guilty.

e.g. *a verdict of not guilty.*

finding judgment sentence

**2.** If you give a verdict on something, you give your opinion after thinking about it.

e.g. *The critics may have hated the film, but the public verdict was favourable.*

conclusion decision judgment opinion

### very

(adverb) Very is used before words to emphasize them.

e.g. *very bad dreams.*

exceedingly extremely highly particularly really remarkably terribly unusually wonderfully

### victory

(noun) A victory is a success in a battle or competition.

e.g. *a crushing victory over her opponents.*

conquest mastery success triumph win

## view

**1.** (noun) Your views are your personal opinions.

e.g. *He went to jail for his political views.*

    attitude  belief  feeling  impression  opinion
    sentiment

**2.** A view is everything you can see from a particular place.

e.g. *Her flat looked out onto a superb view of London.*

    aspect  landscape  outlook  panorama  prospect
    scene  vista

## viewpoint

(noun) Your viewpoint is your attitude towards something.

e.g. *The film looks at the world from a child's viewpoint.*

    outlook  perspective  point of view  position
    stance  standpoint  view

## villain

(noun) A villain is someone who harms others or breaks the law.

e.g. *He had to tackle an armed villain single-handed.*

    blackguard  criminal  knave  miscreant  reprobate
    rogue  scoundrel  wretch

## virtue

**1.** (noun) Virtue is thinking and doing what is morally right and avoiding what is wrong.

e.g. *a priest of great virtue.*

    goodness  integrity  morality  probity  rectitude

**2.** A virtue of something is an advantage.

e.g. *The plan has the virtue of simplicity.*

advantage asset attribute merit strength

## virtuous

(adjective) behaving with or showing moral virtue.

e.g. *a noble and virtuous existence.*

blameless excellent exemplary good honest moral pure righteous upright worthy

## vital

(adjective) necessary or very important.

e.g. *vital evidence.*

cardinal critical crucial decisive essential imperative indispensable key significant

## vivacious

(adjective) A vivacious person is attractively lively and high-spirited.

e.g. *Laura was a vivacious, intelligent woman.*

animated ebullient effervescent exuberant lively sparkling spirited

## vivid

(adjective) very bright in colour or clear in detail.

e.g. *vivid memories.*

clear descriptive distinct glowing graphic intense powerful strong

## vulnerable

(adjective) weak and without protection.

e.g. *Its aim is to keep vulnerable young people off the streets.*

defenceless exposed susceptible unprotected

# _W w_

## wake

(verb) When you wake or when something wakes you, you become conscious again after being asleep.

e.g. _A good night's sleep is essential if we are to wake refreshed._

arouse  awake  awaken  rouse  stir  waken  wake up

## wander

(verb) If you wander in a place, you walk around in a casual way.

e.g. _Visitors are free to wander around the gardens._

drift  meander  ramble  roam  rove  straggle stray  stroll

## war

**1.** (noun) A war is a period of fighting between countries or states when weapons are used and many people may be killed.

e.g. _The president was broadcasting within hours of the outbreak of war._

battle  conflict  fighting  fray  warfare

**2.** (verb) When two countries war with each other, they are fighting a war against each other.

e.g. _They warred with each other for supremacy._

battle  clash  combat  contend  fight  struggle

wage war

## warn

(verb) If you warn someone about a possible problem or danger, you tell them about it in advance so that they are aware of it.

e.g. *I warned him what it would be like.*

alert  caution  forewarn  give notice  tip off

## waste

**I.** (verb) If you waste time, money, or energy, you use too much of it on something that is not important or necessary.

e.g. *If only he wouldn't waste his money on crazy cars.*

dissipate  exhaust  fritter  misuse  squander

**2.** (noun) Waste is the use of more money or some other resource than is necessary.

e.g. *It's a waste of our time and energy.*

dissipation  extravagance  prodigality  profligacy
squandering  wastage

## wasteful

(adjective) extravagant or causing waste by using resources in a careless and inefficient way.

e.g. *a wasteful use of the planet's resources.*

extravagant  improvident  prodigal  profligate
ruinous  spendthrift  uneconomical

## wave

**I.** (verb) If you wave something, you hold it up and move it from side to side.

e.g. *The doctor waved a piece of paper at him.*

brandish  flourish  flutter  shake  wag  wield

**2.** (noun) A wave is a ridge of water on the surface of the sea.

e.g. *lines of white foam where the waves broke on the beach.*

billow  breaker  ripple  roller  swell

**3.** A wave of a feeling is a steady increase in it which spreads through you or through a group of people.

e.g. *a wave of panic.*

outbreak  rush  surge  upsurge

## way

**1.** (noun) A way of doing something is how it is done.

e.g. *different ways of cooking fish.*

fashion  manner  means  method  mode
procedure  process  system

**2.** The way to a particular place is the route that you take to get there.

e.g. *The tourists often get lost on their way to their hotels.*

approach  course  direction  path  road  route

## weak

**1.** (adjective) not having much strength.

e.g. *weak from lack of sleep.*

debilitated  exhausted  faint  feeble  infirm  puny
spent  wasted  weedy

**2.** Someone who is weak is easily influenced by other people.

e.g. *incompetent and weak leadership.*

cowardly effete impotent indecisive irresolute
pathetic shaky soft spineless

## weaken

(verb) If something weakens you, it causes you to lose
some of your physical strength and energy.

e.g. *Toxins in the environment weaken our immune
systems.*

debilitate enervate sap tire undermine

## wealth

(noun) Wealth is the large amount of money,
property, or other valuable things which someone
owns.

e.g. *the attainment of great wealth and property.*

affluence assets fortune means opulence
prosperity resources riches substance
wealthiness

## wealthy

(adjective) having a large amount of money, property,
or other valuable things.

e.g. *a wealthy sugar plantation owner.*

affluent comfortable moneyed opulent
prosperous rich well-off well-to-do

## weird

(adjective) strange or bizarre.

e.g. *a weird religious cult.*

bizarre eerie ghostly grotesque mysterious
odd outlandish queer strange uncanny
unearthly unnatural

## whim

(noun) A whim is a sudden desire or fancy.

e.g. *He uses his money to indulge his every whim.*

caprice fancy humour impulse notion quirk
urge vagary

## whip

(verb) If you whip a person or animal, you hit them
with a whip.

e.g. *I saw him whipping his team of mules.*

beat flay flog lash scourge thrash

## wicked

(adjective) very bad.

e.g. *a wicked thing to do.*

amoral atrocious corrupt evil fiendish heinous
iniquitous nefarious shameful sinful vicious vile

## wide

(adjective) If there is a wide variety, range, or
selection of something, there are many different kinds
of it.

e.g. *a wide range of colours.*

ample broad catholic comprehensive extensive
general vast wide-ranging

## widespread

(adjective) existing or happening over a large area or
to a great extent.

e.g. *the widespread use of chemicals.*

extensive general prevalent rampant rife
sweeping universal wholesale

## wilful

(adjective) Someone who is wilful is obstinate and determined to get their own way.

e.g. *a wilful child.*

> headstrong obstinate perverse self-willed
> stubborn wayward

## willing

(adjective) If you are willing to do something, you will do it if someone wants you to.

e.g. *They are willing to make concessions.*

> agreeable content disposed eager game
> *informal* happy prepared ready

## winner

(noun) The winner of a prize, race, or competition is the person or thing that wins it.

e.g. *the winner of the Grand National.*

> champ champion conqueror first master victor

## wise

(adjective) Someone who is wise can use their experience and knowledge to make sensible decisions and judgments.

e.g. *a very wise and intelligent young lady.*

> discerning enlightened erudite informed
> intelligent judicious perceptive sagacious sage
> shrewd

## wish

1. (noun) A wish is a desire for something.

e.g. *She had no wish to argue.*

> desire hankering inclination longing urge

**2.** (verb) If you wish to do something, you want to do it.

e.g. *He did not wish to go.*

   desire  long  need  want

## witchcraft

(noun) Witchcraft is the skill or art of using magic powers, especially evil ones.

e.g. *a study of witchcraft and magic in early Britain.*

   black magic  sorcery  wizardry

## wither

(verb) When something withers or withers away, it becomes weaker until it no longer exists.

e.g. *Farmers in the Midwest have watched their crops wither because of drought conditions.*

   atrophy  decay  decline  droop  fade  languish
   perish  shrivel  wane  waste away  wilt

## witness

(noun) A witness is someone who has seen an event such as an accident and can describe what happened.

e.g. *I was a witness in a court case a couple of months ago.*

   bystander  eyewitness  observer  onlooker
   spectator

## wonder

**1.** (noun) A wonder is something or someone that surprises or amazes people.

e.g. *the wonders of modern technology.*

   marvel  miracle  phenomenon  prodigy  rarity
   sight  spectacle

**2.** Wonder is a feeling of surprise or amazement.

e.g. *her look of wonder the first time it snowed.*

    admiration astonishment awe bewilderment
    curiosity surprise

## wonderful

(adjective) very impressive.

e.g. *Nature is a wonderful thing.*

    amazing astounding extraordinary magnificent
    marvellous miraculous wondrous

## wood

(noun) A wood is a large area of trees growing near
each other.

e.g. *Follow the road until you reach a wood on your right.*

    copse forest grove thicket woodland

## work

**1.** (noun) Work is a job you are paid to do.

e.g. *I can't find work.*

    business calling employment job line
    occupation profession trade

**2.** Work is things that have to be done.

e.g. *I've got loads of work to do.*

    assignment chore drudgery duty job task

**3.** (verb) If someone works a machine, they control
or operate it.

e.g. *Do you know how to work this video recorder?.*

    control direct drive handle manage manipulate
    move operate ply use

**4.** If something such as an idea or a system works, it

is successful.

e.g. *The housing benefit system is not working.*

    function  go  perform  run

## worried

(adjective) unhappy and anxious about a problem or about something unpleasant that might happen.

e.g. *I'm worried about how long he's taking to finish this job.*

    anxious  apprehensive  bothered  concerned
    distraught  distressed  perturbed  troubled
    uneasy  upset

## worry

**1.** (verb) If you worry, you feel anxious, fearful, and uneasy about a problem or about something unpleasant that might happen.

e.g. *Don't worry, Andrew, you can do it.*

    agonize  fret

**2.** If something worries you, it causes you to feel uneasy or fearful.

e.g. *a puzzle which had worried her all her life.*

    alarm  bother  concern  distress  disturb  perturb
    torment  trouble  unsettle

**3.** (noun) Worry is a feeling of unhappiness and unease caused by a problem or by thinking of something unpleasant that might happen.

e.g. *a major source of worry.*

    anxiety  apprehension  concern  disquiet

## worsen

(verb) If a situation worsens or if something worsens it, it becomes more difficult, unpleasant, or unacceptable.

e.g. *Oil pollution seems to be worsening.*

aggravate compound decline degenerate
deteriorate exacerbate sink

## worship

**1.** (verb) If you worship someone or something, you love them or admire them very much.

e.g. *I went on a trip to Hollywood and saw how they worship old cars over there.*

adore idolize revere venerate

**2.** (noun) Worship is the feeling of respect, love, or admiration you feel for something or someone.

e.g. *rock stars treated as objects of worship.*

adoration adulation devotion homage reverence
veneration

## wrestle

(verb) When you wrestle with a problem, you try to deal with it.

e.g. *For decades mathematicians have wrestled with this problem.*

battle fight grapple strive struggle

## wrinkle

(noun) Wrinkles are lines in someone's skin, especially on the face, which form as they grow old.

e.g. *a new anti-wrinkle cream.*

crease fold furrow line

### wrong

1. (adjective) not correct or truthful.

e.g. *the wrong answer.*

> erroneous   false   inaccurate   incorrect   mistaken
> unsound   untrue

2. not working properly or unsatisfactory.

e.g. *There was nothing wrong with his eyesight.*

> amiss   awry   defective   faulty

3. bad or immoral.

e.g. *It is wrong to steal.*

> bad   dishonest   evil   immoral   sinful   unfair
> unjust   unlawful   wicked   wrongful

### wry

(adjective) A wry expression shows that you find a
situation slightly amusing because you know more
about it than other people.

e.g. *She cast a wry glance in Mary Ann's direction.*

> ironic   mocking   quizzical   sarcastic   sardonic

# *Y y*

**young**

   **1.** (adjective) A young person, animal, or plant has not lived very long and is not yet mature.

   e.g. *You're too young to start smoking.*

       immature  juvenile  youthful

   **2.** (noun) The young of an animal are its babies.

   e.g. *She was like a tigress defending her young.*

       issue  offspring  progeny

VEITCH,
33 GILMOUR
COURT.
PITTENHAR